DAVID WATSON is Dir...
Brighton. He previously taught at Crewe and
Alsager College of Higher Education and Oxford
Polytechnic, and has published widely on the
history of ideas and higher education policy. He
is the author of *Margaret Fuller: An American
Romantic* (1988), *Managing the Modular Course*
(1989) and *Developing Professional Education*
(1992).

MODERN MASTERS

BARTHES	Jonathan Culler
BECKETT	Al Alvarez
CHOMSKY	John Lyons
DERRIDA	Christopher Norris
DURKHEIM	Anthony Giddens
EINSTEIN	Jeremy Bernstein
ELIOT	Stephen Spender
FOUCAULT	JG Merquior
FREUD	Richard Wollheim
HEIDEGGER	George Steiner
JUNG	Anthony Storr
LACAN	Malcolm Bowie
LAWRENCE	Frank Kermode
MARX	David McLellan
NIETZSCHE	JP Stern
ORWELL	Raymond Williams
POPPER	Bryan Magee
PROUST	Roger Shattuck
SARTRE	Arthur C. Danto
SAUSSURE	Jonathan Culler
WEBER	Donald MacRae
WINNICOTT	Adam Phillips
WITTGENSTEIN	David Pears

Forthcoming:

BENJAMIN	Samuel Weber
BERLIN	John Gray

Arendt

DAVID WATSON

FontanaPress
An Imprint of HarperCollins*Publishers*

First published in 1992 by Fontana Press,
an imprint of HarperCollins*Publishers*
77–85 Fulham Palace Road
Hammersmith, London W6 8JB

1 3 5 7 9 8 6 4 2

© David Watson 1992

David Watson asserts the moral right to be
identified as the author of this work

A catalogue record for this book is
available from the British Library

ISBN 0 00 686237 3

All rights reserved

Printed and bound in Great Britain by
HarperCollinsManufacturing Glasgow

CONDITIONS OF SALE

This book is sold subject to the condition that it
shall not by trade or otherwise, be lent, re-
sold, hired out or otherwise circulated without the
publisher's prior consent in any form of binding or
cover other than that in which it is published and
without a similar condition being imposed on the
subsequent purchaser.

In memoriam

Lewis James Watson (1911–1985)

Contents

Acknowledgements	9
Preface	11

PART I
Europe: *The Experience of Totalitarianism*

1. Early Life	19
2. Higher Education	26
3. The Flight from Nazism	34

PART II
Israel: *The Political Necessity of Zionism*

4. Arendt and Zionism	65
5. *Eichmann in Jerusalem*	74

PART III
America: *From Political Theory to Philosophy*

6. Arendt and the American Republic	85
7. *The Life of the Mind*	105
Postscript	121
References	127
Bibliography	137

Acknowledgements

I owe to my former colleague Peter Madgwick the reassuring insight that large subjects can be served by little books. Certainly doing justice to the range and significance of Hannah Arendt's life and work within the compass of a brief introductory volume has proved a humbling task. Like most authors of little books I am, of course, indebted to the writers of other, big books. My chief guide has been Arendt's former student Elisabeth Young-Bruehl in her magnificent 'philosophical biography', *Hannah Arendt: For Love of the World* (1982). Young-Bruehl combines a sensitive and comprehensive account of the life with an engaged exposition of the work. Most of her judgements I share; those few which I do not continue to worry me.

Closer to home, I am deeply appreciative of those friends and colleagues who have read, listened to and influenced my evolving and still incomplete understanding of Arendt's life and work. These include participants in the Sociology Staff Seminar and the RAW LAW (Reading and Writing in Law) group at Oxford Polytechnic, as well as the 1990 History of Ideas Colloquium held at Brighton Polytechnic. Bruce Kuklick, Frank Webster, Roger Griffin, Sir Frank Kermode and Rebecca Wilson patiently read and commented on the manuscript. So, too, did Betty Skolnick, whose family history embodies many of the key issues which moved Arendt's political and philosophical speculations. Sarah and Michael Watson were equally encouraging.

The various overlapping versions of the manuscript were typed, logged and ordered with her usual meticulous care by Cheryl Codling. I am deeply indebted to her, and to the efficient library services of Oxford Polytechnic and Cambridge University. An earlier version of parts of Chapters Six and Seven was published in *The Transactions of the Charles S. Peirce Society*.

David Watson
Brighton
March 1992

Preface

Hannah Arendt was the author of two of the most controversial works in western intellectual discourse of the 1950s and 1960s: *The Origins of Totalitarianism* (first published in 1951) and *Eichmann in Jerusalem* (which first appeared in book form in 1963, a year after the state of Israel executed Adolf Eichmann, but which caused a furore well before publication). Both deal, although in dramatically different ways, with the major political, social, and above all moral crises of the century. In their day, they were enormously successful (if one measures this in terms of sales, the number of translations, the extent of public controversy, and so on). But neither has lasted particularly well.

As a thinker and a person Hannah Arendt inspired during her life intense hostility and equally intense loyalty. Her critics characteristically conflate the person and her work in varying styles of dismissal. Some of these opinions tune in well with more 'academic' judgements which have been expressed about Arendt. Isaiah Berlin told Derwent May, when the latter was preparing his short study for Penguin, that 'she doesn't get a single fact about Russia right.'[1] Similarly, Anthony Quinton concludes his brief and damning entry in the *Fontana Biographical Companion to Modern Thought* by describing her unfinished *The Life of the Mind* as having 'adopted a grandly systematic posture which its elusive content did little to sustain'.[2] For Stuart

Hampshire the same work is an example of 'metaphysical mists', and a severe case of American self-delusion.[3]

It is easy, but misleading, to suggest that what is happening here is a convergence between two powerful forces in modern western intellectual life: Jewish outrage at what was perceived as Arendt's treachery in qualifying Nazi responsibility for the Holocaust (in part by pointing to the 'banality' of Eichmann's evil actions, and in part by hinting at the complicity of some Jews in their own destruction); and Oxford-based academic snobbery.

Both criticisms can be justified to a certain extent. Arendt was, for example, compelled to revise some of her more extreme views in *Eichmann in Jerusalem* in the face of inconvenient facts, although she was rarely prepared to acknowledge these retractions beyond the adjustments made to subsequent editions. Equally, her style of argument made few concessions to her detractors. She proudly eschewed the kind of equivocation and careful qualification of her ideas that might have made the statements in this book palatable, or at least seem less like a betrayal. Similarly, her political, historical, and philosophical writings (for some almost perversely) resist categorization along traditional lines. She was neither rigorous, consistent nor accurate in the ways that Berlin, Quinton and others would regard as prerequisites for serious consideration.

Another way to measure these problems is by the extensive disclaimers which her defenders feel it necessary to make before proceeding with any constructive account of her work. Margaret Canovan, for example, concedes that 'her whole technique is a social scientist's nightmare' and that to penetrate fully her 'particular and unusual understanding of the business of politics and the business of thinking' a number of traditional critical criteria have to be suspended.[4] Melvyn Hill similarly points to her 'peculiar reputation': 'while her books are respected, few people feel comfortable with the way she argues or with the conclusions she reached.'[5] Supportive studies of Arendt nearly always begin by saying, 'you have to make allowances', while critical studies are backed up by her uncompromising and occasionally petulant response to questions and criticism.[6]

Despite these difficulties of classification almost all studies of Arendt identify and discuss her as a political theorist. This is, after all, what she claimed to be and it is where most of the controversies settle. Her use of empirical evidence was uncertain and subject to occasionally damaging corrections. She also made unusual use of linguistic and semantic distinctions. Like some other more revered figures in the history of political thought (for example, her life-long antagonist Leo Strauss) she took pleasure in using words in unconventional senses, creating a system that refers to nothing outside itself which readers could grasp.[7] Some commentators, like C. B. Macpherson, find this weakness close to fatal, tempting her into 'outrageous' statements such as 'Marx didn't understand power.'[8] Arendt also developed an idiosyncratic dialectic of thought and action. She held that the political theorist should never prescribe – leading to the situation where, in the words of Richard Bernstein, 'concerning the issue of what is to be done, the theorist must always be silent.'[9] Finally, perhaps most critically, she was exposed by a selective use of the political-theoretical tradition, in particular her personal understanding of societies such as fifth-century Athens, revolutionary America, and the modern USSR.

Identifying Arendt as a political theorist is reinforced by several experiences in her life: her personal experience as a refugee from totalitarianism; the Jewish perspective, not only culturally (the 'pariah' vs. 'parvenu' dichotomy she began to think about with her life of Rahel Varnhagen), but also politically with her Zionist work and her support, albeit conditional, for the state of Israel (her biographer Elisabeth Young-Bruehl points to Arendt's crucial realization in the early 1930s that 'when one is attacked as a Jew, one must defend oneself as a Jew'); the discovery in the United States of constitutional protections for the individual; and, in the final years of her life, the ambiguities of the Cold War and the various attempts at human liberation inspired by 1968.[10] All this evidence can be adduced to give a meaning to Arendt's work in terms of a critique of traditional political philosophy and the articulation of an alternative. It has also meant that elements which do not fit can be identified as defects.

In my view the critique of Arendt as a political theorist fails mainly because it seeks a kind of unity (in method, motive and/or outcome) for her political thought. Each of the interpretations cited finds this, up to a point, and then lists where it falls short. Arendt is frequently shown to have failed to provide a coherent account of political man, political society, and/or political goals.

My own interest in Arendt is influenced by this feeling of uncomfortableness. On the one hand I can approach her work armed with all of the academic objections to its validity. As scholarship, for example, *The Origins of Totalitarianism* is massively flawed. On the other hand, in addition to the book's idiosyncratic intellectual challenge, I find questions within the work which are unique and which are addressed in a way that often has an affective impact. My approach looks at her political theory obliquely, combines the work and the life, and suggests a different set of goals – more faithful, I would claim, to the firm scepticism Arendt frequently expressed about the methods and results of 'behavioural social science'. A key problem for Arendt (and for us) is, I think, how to achieve philosophical detachment in the twentieth century, leading on to questions not only about how to assign responsibility for individual and group actions but also about how an individual qualifies himself or herself to judge these actions. This is the principal focus of my exposition of Arendt's work, as well as the explanation of why, despite her repudiation of the role, I choose finally to identify her as a philosopher.

Adopting this approach implies concentrating, unfashionably, on the later and in particular the posthumously published work, and analysing the earlier and more successful books (the *Origins*, *The Human Condition* (1958), *On Revolution* (1963), as well as *Eichmann*) in terms of the philosophical ground they cleared. It also explains the otherwise unexpected way in which I have juxtaposed Arendt's life and work in the chapters that follow. In several phases of her life Arendt systematically 'worked through' problems she had previously and personally experienced. Her final effort of this sort, *The Life of the Mind*, was tragically unfinished. In the Postscript I return to the question of her reputation and the enduring value of her work.

PART I

Europe:

THE EXPERIENCE OF TOTALITARIANISM

CHAPTER ONE

Early Life

Hannah Arendt was born in 1906 in Hanover, into a relatively prosperous middle-class Jewish family. Her parents were representative of a group of professional families who, while not assimilated into German gentile society, participated in mildly liberal politics. They were members of the Social Democratic Party, and Hannah recalls being taken by her mother to observe a Spartacist rally during the 'revolution' of 1919. They held no particular common cause with the more recent Jewish immigrants from the East. As an only child she was brought up with touching care and attention, reflected by the diary ('Unser Kind' – our child) which her mother Martha kept up into Hannah's teens.

Family life was, however, overshadowed by tragedy. Hannah's father Paul, an engineer, had contracted syphilis and the cure thought to be complete before his marriage had failed. When Hannah was four she returned with her parents to Königsberg in East Prussia (the birthplace and home of Immanuel Kant – the philosophical hero of her adult life), where Paul could receive treatment. He was in effect an invalid throughout the period during which she knew him. In 1913 he died, and so did his father Max Arendt who had been a much-loved and effective surrogate during Hannah's infancy. Mother and daughter were thrown together in a tangle of dependence and concern which they found difficult to acknowledge. Other traumas also intruded as the family was forced to flee to Berlin in the face of the Russian army in the first offensive of World War I in 1914.

In 1920, out of concern for the material and psychological welfare of her daughter, Martha married an elderly widower Martin Beerwald, and Hannah moved in with them and two older stepsisters, Clara and Eva, with whom she maintained an affectionate but slightly distant relationship. In her teens her friends were largely from outside the family and connected with school and her burgeoning intellectual interests. Two stand out: Anne Mendelssohn (later Weil), who remained a touchstone for this phase of her life and the origins which they shared, and Ernst Grumach, who encouraged her to set up a kind of intellectual salon in her room at the Beerwalds'.

Hannah's school work was recognized as brilliant, but she also developed a reputation for independence and rebelliousness. She was in fact expelled from school a year before she was due to take her *Abitur* or leaving examination, after she had led a boycott against a teacher whom she claimed had insulted her. Instead, she studied privately for the examination at the University of Berlin, with the slightly bemused support of her new family. In 1925 she passed with distinction.

Arendt's childhood and teenage years thus reflected both the apparent peace and tranquillity of the early Weimar era and the contradictions this posed for the Jewish middle class. There was also a degree of personal turmoil. The former structured many of the concerns of her mature working life, beginning with the life of Rahel Varnhagen which she began to work on as a post-graduate student. The latter is encapsulated in some of her youthful poems and a brief autobiographical fragment written when she was at university in 1925.

'Die Schatten'

'Die Schatten' ('the shadows') was written for Arendt's university teacher, Martin Heidegger. She was nineteen and he thirty-five, and they were nearing the end of an intense affair. Writing from home in Königsberg she attempted a psychological self-portrait, explaining her background and what their relationship meant to her. On a superficial level, it gives a picture of a frozen, unfulfilled personality released by love and the 'unbending devotion to a single one'. More deeply, it validates other impressions of Arendt as a child, and explains the intellectual as well as emotional single-mindedness which she took with her into adult life.

In describing herself Arendt acknowledged her reputation as a 'sunshine child' (a term of her mother's), but also noted her propensity to discover the strange and the magical in events and things around her. She talked about being habitually bewildered and yet fascinated by reality in a way which suggested she was under a 'spell'. The pain over her father's death, although not explicitly mentioned, must have contributed to this. In Heideggerian terms, she referred to it as 'anxiety over existence in general'.

The relationship with Heidegger was indeed a watershed for Arendt, but by writing about it in the past tense she showed her realization that it could not last. His family and career would carry him away, although he always acknowledged what she had brought into his life during one of its most creative periods. (Their letters have been preserved, but are not available to scholars.) The affair had changed her and recharged her youthful love of life, but she also recognized that the *Bann* or spell which made her fearful and inquisitive would endure.

A year later, in Freiburg, Arendt wrote what Elizabeth Young-Bruehl (whose translation this is) refers to as 'one of the best of her poems', including these stanzas:

> I no longer know how love feels
> I no longer know the fields aglow
> And everything wants to drift away –
> Simply to give me peace.
>
> I think of him and of the love –
> As though it were a distant land;
> And the 'come and give' is foreign
> I hardly know what bound me.[1]

'Die Schatten' was a psychological and personal attempt by Arendt to come to terms with her identity and her origins. Later, as a post-graduate student, she expanded and made more critical these sociological and historical insights in her study of the life of Rahel Varnhagen.

Rahel Varnhagen

Arendt began work on the papers and letters of Rahel Varnhagen in the late 1920s having been introduced to the subject by her friend Anne Mendelssohn. She was particularly attracted to the letters which had been expurgated or suppressed in the accounts published by Varnhagen's husband. By 1933 all but the last two chapters of the book, eventually published in 1957, had been completed.

The project was born of empathy with her subject's social

EARLY LIFE

and psychological situation, and led to a barely concealed projection of Arendt's own anxieties and sensitivities about growing up as a Jew and as a romantic in a society whose toleration of both characteristics was at best ambiguous. In Arendt's words, 'what interested me solely was to narrate the story of Rahel's life as she herself might have told it.'[2] For Young-Bruehl the work completed the exorcism begun in 'Die Schatten'. She quotes Arendt's description of 'my closest friend, though she has been dead for some one hundred years'.[3]

Varnhagen herself was a Jewess who had presided over a salon in early nineteenth-century Berlin, catering to many famous literary figures including Schleiermacher, Schlegel, and Von Humboldt. Throughout her life she explored the dilemma on which Arendt later based her analysis of choices available to Jews in modern society: to assimilate as a 'parvenu' or remain a 'pariah'. Rahel overcame agonies of rejection and loneliness before she finally married the diplomat August Varnhagen, himself a failed medical student and poet whose career benefited from some spectacular strokes of luck. She was simultaneously baptized a Christian. If August's relationship to Rahel was like that of Arendt's to her own first husband, Günther Anders – 'a reliable friend' who understood some of her need for security without fully probing her existential dilemmas – so, too, there is an analogy for Heidegger in Rahel's youthful affair with the unattainable, gentile aristocrat Finkelstein.[4]

As Arendt concluded, however, self-discovery and a kind of peace lay in overcoming assimilation and re-establishing the 'view of the whole' that is the special possession of the pariah: 'that she succeeded in salvaging her pariah qualities when she entered her parvenu existence opened up a loophole for her, marked out a road towards aging and dying'.[5] *Rahel Varnhagen: The Life of a Jewish Woman* is in its final form an almost strictly chronological arrangement of and commentary upon Rahel's letters and papers. In this way Arendt describes her early fears, alliances and love-affairs ('Rahel's struggle against the facts, above all against the fact of having been born a Jew, very rapidly became a struggle against herself'), the success of the salon, a flight to Paris, and the route to assimilation through August who unashamedly took her life and used it to define his own. 'Rahel's life became more human because it now had a pedagogical effect upon another human being.' After her marriage and the sharing of her husband's career it became clear, however, that assimilation was a chimera: 'the bourgeoisie did not accept them, and the nobility drew away from them.' In response, Rahel's self-discovery was painful but profound. She recognized her separation from the 'dark mass of the people', read and admired the early socialist Saint-Simon, rediscovered Hebrew, and returned to her roots. 'It turned out that the pariah was capable not only of preserving more feeling for the "true realities" but that in some circumstances he also possessed more reality than the parvenu.'[6]

On one level Arendt's account of Rahel Varnhagen is a commentary on the strength and weaknesses of the romantic personality. In response to the Enlightenment's striving for rights, members of unassimilated sections of society faced even greater difficulties of guilt and inferiority. As Varnhagen wrote to one of the friends of her youth, quoting Goethe, 'only galley slaves know one another.' One romantic means of escape was that of self-dramatization, of turning one's own life into an exemplary narrative. This was a lesson Rahel learned from Goethe, who later found it exemplified in her case when he read the correspondence.[7] Viewing it from outside, Arendt redefined the problem in existential terms as that of 'being at home in the world'; of establishing the right balance of generality and specificity; and of affirming one's own 'singularity' in the face of the brutal world of 'facts'. Rahel 'resisted accepting a society and a view of the world whose foundations would inevitably always remain hostile to her'.[8]

In time, and especially in *The Origins of Totalitarianism*, the historical perspectives upon which Arendt calls to make sense of Rahel's life were to assume a more theoretical importance for her. These included the unique position of German Jews, whose history was ended with the Holocaust, the preconditions for periodic anti-Semitic outbursts, and the problems of the unassimilable: 'Just as every anti-Semite knew his personal exception Jews in Berlin, so every Berlin Jew knew at least two Eastern Jews in comparison with whom he felt himself to be an exception.'[9] Sociologically, there were periods of respite and it was during one of these that the salon had flourished. However, at this stage in her own evolution the psychological insight was more important to Arendt than the sociological. Rahel's dreams of a room to which she could not gain admission, and her final dignified reconciliation to the insolubility of the Jewish problem, were for her biographer both touching and inspiring.[10]

CHAPTER TWO

Higher Education

In 1924 Arendt left her family home to go to Marburg University, where she became a brilliant undergraduate student of philosophy. Her mentor there was Martin Heidegger, with whom she had the affair during 1925 which inspired 'Die Schatten'. Her subsequent relationship with Heidegger, who in 1933 was appointed Rector of Freiburg University by the Nazis, remained a tortuous thread throughout her life as she sought to explain herself to him, and him to the outside world. Largely as a consequence of the aftermath of this affair, she switched universities for her post-graduate studies, moving to Heidelberg where she worked with Karl Jaspers. Jaspers was to remain an opposing pole to Heidegger in her relationship to German political and philosophical life. In the 1960s she collected and published his papers in a book called *The Great Philosophers*.

As a student, Arendt benefited from the flexibility and the sense of a new beginning in philosophy which animated the German university system at the time. She also spent a semester in 1925 studying at Freiburg with Husserl. Certain friendships begun when she was a student were to become permanent fixtures in her life, particularly those with the philosopher Hans Jonas and the Zionist leader Kurt Blumenfeld. Blumenfeld had been a close friend of Arendt's grandfather and had first met her as a child in Königsberg.

Other relationships she had with, for example, the poet Erich Loewensen and a fellow student Benno von Wiese, were more romantic. In January 1929 she met her first husband, Günther Stern, at a fancy-dress party in Berlin. She subsequently moved there where Stern helped her in the final work on her doctoral thesis, and where they were married. In September they moved to Frankfurt where Stern hoped to begin an academic career. In the same year Arendt's thesis on the concept of love in the works of St Augustine was published to general acclaim. It is still regularly cited in theological research. Thus by the end of her formal education, and armed with a grant to work on the history of German romanticism (which supported her early work on Rahel Varnhagen), Arendt was poised for a career as a university teacher and researcher herself.

St Augustine and the concept of love

Arendt's doctoral dissertation, *Der Leibesbegriffe bei Augustin*, is, to the reader attracted by much of her mature work, an austere and forbidding exercise. It deals with its subject in strict 'philosophical' terms, as set by Heidegger and Jaspers. It was not until the mid-1960s, when Arendt briefly contemplated revising the manuscript for publication and a translation was mooted, that she considered in detail how the argument could be made more accessible to those with a less detailed knowledge of her work. In what follows I am guided by a sensitive and illuminating 'synopsis' prepared by Young-Bruehl as an appendix to *For Love of the World*.[1]

The main achievement of the work is to show how, beginning from a variety of definitions of desire and an analysis of their uses, Augustine is led into dead ends and dilemmas. These include not only the base desires such as 'craving' (*appetitus*), the desire for worldly goods (*cupiditas*) and even a selfish desire for eternity, but also 'self-love', with its dilemma of temporality (man should presumably love his future, eternal self more than his contingent, sinful present self), and the key concept of 'neighbourly love' (*caritas*). The result of observing the commandment 'Love thy neighbour as thyself' (the foundation stone of the City of God) can degenerate in a circular fashion into self-interest.

Running through these dilemmas is, for Arendt, the problem of knowledge. In Young-Bruehl's words:

> The happy life, if it is to be the object of desire, must be known; but if this is so knowledge must precede desire, knowledge must present the object of desire. Put in another way: past knowledge is the basis for a projection into the future. Desire transcends the present toward the future, but it can do so only because memory transcends the present, guarding the past.[2]

In time this was to become one of Arendt's most enduring themes: understanding through retrospection as the basis for responsible behaviour. In notes made in 1963 she also linked this facility of conscious remembering with the philosophical understanding of birth and death ('natality', or beginning, and 'mortality', at once feared and anticipated positively as the opportunity for immortality). But these themes in her mature work are as much political as philosophical. In an indirect way Augustine was raising questions about history and freedom which Arendt sought later to develop in *The Human Condition*.

Augustine was a persistent force in Arendt's canon of landmark figures in the intellectual history of the West.

According to Alfred Kazin, 'she had devoted herself to Augustine because of a single sentence: "Love means that I want you to be".'³ In the work of some commentators, this reinforces the tendency to overemphasize her attraction to the Christian religion. It is true that Augustine's view of the conscience, together with traditional Christian doctrines such as redemption and atonement, feature centrally in her later concepts of judgement and forgiveness. But, as her more mature works indicate, Arendt's version of *caritas*, the love that creates a common world, was unashamedly secular.

The philosophy of 'Existenz'

Writing in 1964 in response to Gershom Scholem's open letter on the publication of *Eichmann in Jerusalem*, which included the accusation that she lacked sympathy 'as in so many intellectuals who came from the German left', Arendt was quick to redefine her origins: 'If I can be said to "have come from anywhere" it is from the tradition of German philosophy.'⁴ It is important to 'fix' this claim, rooted as it was in Arendt's experience of higher education, in order to appreciate her most secure points of reference throughout her intellectual career.

There are two broad currents in modern German philosophy, each of which can be traced back to the greatest modern philosopher, Immanuel Kant. The first leads through idealist metaphysics and a developing historicism from Herder, Fichte and Schelling to Hegel. This current emerges in Marx's dialectical materialism, standing on its head the full-blown absolute idealism of Hegel. The second current detours through the thought of Kierkegaard, the father of existentialism, and returns in the tradition of Husserl, Heidegger and Jaspers. Its contemporary destination is the modern tradition of phenomenology and hermeneutics.

Before she was overwhelmed by politics, totalitarianism and enforced migration to America, Arendt absorbed certain problems, priorities and techniques from her teachers and her peers which survived almost unscathed for the rest of her life. First and foremost, this included a canon of major periods and writers with three distinct but reinforcing poles: the use of the classical world (Greece more than Rome) as a testing ground for moral and political propositions; the early Christian (and Roman) philosophical advances made by Augustine, particularly in the area of personal responsibility; and, finally, a pantheon of modern philosophical heroes, the founders of the genuinely 'existential' tradition – Kant, Kierkegaard, Husserl and Heidegger. Interestingly, the canon excludes at this stage both Hegel and Marx. The latter she did not begin to confront until she went to America and began writing *The Human Condition*; the former was reserved for serious attention until the last years of her life, the Gifford Lectures and *The Life of the Mind*.

From this canon Arendt derived a fixed position on a number of issues that her later work interpreted and reinterpreted but never seriously challenged or set aside. Chief among these were the superiority of Greek politics, especially through its attribute of political beginnings (which she termed 'natality'), the Augustinian doctrine of the will, and the idea of individual 'being' or 'existenz'. In one of her first major philosophical articles in America, 'What is Existenz Philosophy?' (1946), she defined *Existenz* as the 'being of man, independent of all qualities and capacities that can be psychologically investigated'.[5]

In many ways this article is an early answer to the question of what Arendt meant when she said that she came from the tradition of German philosophy. That tradition had tackled a central problem in modern philosophy – the breaking apart of essence and existence, of human identity and the world in which it exists. Another way of stating this is 'how to come to terms with the fact that man is not the creator of the world'. The problem was most clearly articulated by Kant, and equally clearly evaded by Hegel, who is described here as 'the last ancient philosopher'.

> The unity of Being and thought presupposed the pre-established coincidence of essence and existence, that, namely, everything thinkable also exists and every existent, because it is knowable, must also be rational. This unity was destroyed by Kant, the true, if clandestine, founder of the new philosophy: who has likewise remained till the present time its secret king.[6]

Kant's work on the structure and processes of Reason broke down a feeling of security in the oneness of Being that had been absorbed from ancient into Christian philosophy, and simultaneously raised and lowered man's sense of his own capacities.

> While Kant made man the master and measure of Man, at the same time he lowered him to a slave of Being. Every new philosopher since Schelling has protested against this devaluation. Modern philosophy is still occupied with this reduction of Man who had just come of age.[7]

Further implications were developed by Kierkegaard from this base of radical subjectivity. His melancholic philosophy starts from the 'forlornness of the individual in the completely explained world', and confronts the paradox of the individual trying to grasp universal truth. The result is a catalogue of 'existential' insights:

> *Death* as the guarantee of the *principium individuationis*, since death, as the most common of occurrences, nevertheless strikes one unavoidably alone, *Contingency* as guarantee of reality as only given, which overwhelms and persuades us precisely through its incalculability and irreducibility to thought. *Guilt* as the category of all human activity, which is wrecked not upon the world but upon itself, in so far as I always take responsibilities upon myself which I cannot overlook, and am compelled through any decisions themselves to neglect other activity.[8]

Against this tradition Arendt then compares her two most important contemporary influences: Heidegger and Jaspers. At this stage Heidegger, despite his heroic attempt to re-establish the ontology destroyed by Kant and Kierkegaard and his achievement of the 'first absolutely and uncompromisingly this-worldly philosophy', comes off worse. Through his philosophy man is encouraged to grasp his own 'Existenz' by 'being-in-the-world'. However, the self thus created is fundamentally flawed in its 'absolute egoism' and its 'radical separation from all its fellows'.[9] Jaspers supplies this lack by rediscovering the drive to communication, freedom, and spontaneity. In this way the 'search for an ontology is liquidated'. Instead, the individual can discover the limits of his freedom in 'extreme situations' and pass from mere Being to self-knowing 'Existenz'.

> Existenz itself is never essentially isolated; it exists only in communication and in the knowledge of the Existenz of

others. One's fellow men are not (as in Heidegger) an element which, though structurally necessary, nevertheless destroys Existenz; but, on the contrary, Existenz can develop only in the togetherness of men in the common given world.[10]

'What is Existenz Philosophy?' is a difficult, often awkwardly expressed essay. Arendt had not yet achieved the fluency of her later idiosyncratic American English, and the act of translation is palpable. None the less, it is an important interim commentary on the meaning of the 'German tradition'. The idea of phenomenology as an attempt to master the modern condition of homelessness with which it begins, and that of the escape from egoism with which it ends, inspire statements which focus many of Arendt's enduring concerns. Later she was to overlay these insights with other sources and ideas – American political constitutionalism, New World cultural traits that contrasted with some of these European concerns, and the developed critique of Hegel and Marx – but in accepting these new influences Arendt never retreated from a sense that she was bearing a torch passed to her by her teachers, Heidegger and Jaspers, and their teachers from the Greek and German traditions.

CHAPTER THREE

The Flight from Nazism

In 1933 Günther Stern, who after the failure of his *Habilitation* in Frankfurt (largely through the opposition of Theodor Adorno) had switched careers to journalism, fled to Paris in fear that his name might be linked with opposition groups after the *Reichstag* fire of February. Arendt remained in Berlin, where her apartment became a haven for dissidents escaping Nazi investigation, and began a research project on anti-Semitism for Blumenfeld and the German Zionist Organization. Eventually she was picked up and questioned for over a week, an ordeal which she bore with calm but which convinced her that her days, too, were numbered. In the same year Heidegger became Rector of Freiburg University where he began to enforce the Nazi statutes against Jewish teachers, including his own mentor Husserl.

Later that year Arendt, with her mother, Martha, who had endured her own domestic difficulties with Beerwald's bankruptcy in 1925 and the suicide of her stepdaughter Clara in 1932, began a tortuous flight from the Nazi regime. This took them initially to Prague, and then to Geneva, where Arendt briefly worked as a secretary with the League of Nations and from where Martha returned again to her husband. Finally Arendt, alone, joined Stern in Paris.

Arendt's Paris years were a curious amalgam of intellectual

and cultural stimulation, political activity (this was the height of her Zionist engagement, described in Chapter Five), and impending threat. There she extended her circle of friends (which notably included the critic Walter Benjamin), cemented her relationship with others from her youth such as Lotte Sempel (who eventually married Arendt's Hebrew teacher), and met and married the man who was to be of central importance to both her personal and political life for the next thirty years of her life, Heinrich Blücher.

Once again Stern left Paris before Arendt, moving to New York in 1936, by which time their marriage was in effect over. They were amicably divorced later in the year. Arendt had already fallen in love with Blücher, a non-Jew, who had participated in the Spartarcist rebellion of 1919, and was a founder member of the German Communist Party. His enthusiastically practical approach to history and politics neatly complemented her own thoughts and she consistently characterized her work during his lifetime as a partnership.

Meanwhile, both the political situation and that of Arendt's family became more complex. Eva Beerwald emigrated to England soon after the Austrian *Anschluss* of March 1938, and following the orgy of anti-Jewish violence of the *Kristallnacht* in November of the same year Martha began to reconsider her position. Although Martin Beerwald felt unable to leave his home, where he uneasily survived the war unlike several other members of the Arendt and Beerwald families, Martha left in April 1939 to join her daughter and her lover in Paris.

Arendt and Blücher were eventually married in January 1940, after he too had sorted out a divorce. She may have had their relationship in mind when she wrote of Rosa Luxemburg and Leo Jogiches in *Men in Dark Times*: 'This generation still believed firmly that love strikes only once, and its carelessness with marriage certificates should not be mistaken for any belief in free love.'[1]

This new family unit was before long subject to great stress. In the spring of 1938 the French government had begun to issue anti-alien edicts and by August 1939 they had initiated a programme of interning German nationals. Blücher was briefly arrested but released in November after some complicated representations to the authorities by Lotte Sempel. In May 1940 both he and Arendt were swept up by a general internment order (Martha escaped because of her age). After a week in a stadium in Paris Arendt was sent to a women's camp in Gurs, near the Spanish border. She had no idea of the fate of Blücher who was eventually 'liberated' by Germans and let loose. By this time Arendt too had been freed as a consequence of the fall of France and she met Blücher by chance in the street in Montauban where she had taken a house with friends.

From their subsequent accounts the summer of 1941 spent in Montauban was, despite the French defeat, a period of idyllic rural existence, but it could not last. In October the Vichy government ordered all Jews to register with the police. As a married couple, Arendt and Blücher succeeded in getting visas for the United States and in January 1941 they left for Lisbon. In April they arrived in New York – Arendt with the papers of Walter Benjamin who tragically had failed to escape by a similar route through Spain. In June they were joined by Martha, who two months earlier had finally received her own precious visa.

The Origins of Totalitarianism

The Origins of Totalitarianism is the *summum* of Arendt and Blücher's reflections on what had made them and others exiles.

This immediacy overcomes the fact of its final preparation and publication in the highly-charged atmosphere of the early Cold War years. In the preface to the first edition (1951) Arendt explicitly anticipated a third World War, asserting an 'ill-defined general agreement that the essential structure of all civilizations is at breaking-point'. The 'task of comprehension' to which the book is directed faces both forwards and backwards in time. Seeing her audience oscillate wildly between 'desperate hope' (the 'omnipotence' of utopianism) and 'desperate fear' (or 'powerlessness'), Arendt develops two types of explanation in an attempt to answer fundamental questions about the nature of totalitarian society: 'What happened? Why did it happen? How could it have happened?'[2]

The first explanation is historical and sociological, and sits uncomfortably with the sustained critique of behavioural social science that Arendt later developed in *The Human Condition*. In this mode she attempts to answer questions about the origins and development of terror and domination in mass society – what she calls 'the subterranean stream of western history' which has 'finally come to the surface and usurped the dignity of our tradition'. In the original draft Arendt discussed three main forces of destabilization (three 'pillars of hell') that came together after the watershed of 1914: anti-Semitism, imperialism and racism (Arendt had originally defined totalitarianism as race-imperialism).[3] By the time of publication the second two had been conflated. These destructive forces had been held in precious balance by the European system of nation-states before its sudden collapse and disintegration.

As a second explanation, Arendt attempts a political-theoretical account of the essence of totalitarianism, a new and entirely modern form of domination depending on the erasure of individuality in mass society and the ideology of terror.

> Totalitarianism in power uses the state administration for its long-range goal of world conquest and for the direction of the branches of the movement; it establishes the secret police as the executors and guardians of its domestic experiment in constantly transforming reality into fiction; and it finally erects concentration camps as special laboratories to carry through its experiments in total domination.[4]

Drawing both kinds of analysis together Arendt offers a specific history of the Jewish experience, rejecting the received wisdom of 'eternal antisemitism' as an explanation of the fate of European Jewry. Instead, she proposes a structural analysis of the Jewish role in first creating the possibility of modern nationalism (chiefly through financial services – also important in early imperial adventures) and then apparently threatening it through their supranational identity. This culminates in a detailed account of the Dreyfus affair and its twentieth-century legacy, in particular the Zionist movement: 'the only political answer Jews have ever found to anti-Semitism'.[5]

Methodologically, *The Origins of Totalitarianism* is an odd mixture of styles and techniques. It depends in part on primary material, especially evidence from the Nuremberg trials (which was only just beginning to be released and/or published), but more heavily on a selection of secondary authors, who, once introduced with a favourable comment, are almost invariably relied upon in the bulk of the exposition.[6] Interspersed are testimonies of key literary witnesses, so that, for example, we are given the theory of British imperialism through Kipling, Conrad and T. E. Lawrence.[7]

In emphasizing the novelty of totalitarian government there is also a strong normative element, measuring modern political possibilities against earlier, purer, usually Greek concepts and systems. What prevents the theoretical exposition from becoming remote and abstract is a powerful phenomenological sense of the 'isolation' and 'loneliness' of living under these conditions, feeding as it does on 'uprootedness' and 'superfluousness'. Totalitarianism represents a new beginning in our cumulative experience just as much as any of those experiences of which she approves (like the American Revolution), and it is one which cannot be uninvented: 'The crisis of our time and its central experience have brought forth an entirely new form of government which as a potentiality and an ever present danger is only too likely to stay with us from now on.'[8]

Critically, *The Origins of Totalitarianism* has suffered major damage, especially in the last decade, in both theoretical terms (Margaret Canovan, one of Arendt's champions, concedes considerable weaknesses in its conception of the nation-state), and for its empirical inaccuracy, notably in the case of Russia. Although the thesis depends on seeing Stalinism as developing from Nazism, it is in fact dominated by discussion of Germany, a lack of balance Arendt subsequently admitted herself, especially as events in the USSR after the death of Stalin caused her to reconsider the direction of the regime. In the 1968 edition she acknowledged that Russia was undertaking a process of 'detotalitarianization'.[9] Probably more important is the book's historiographical significance as the first and weightiest synthesis in the English language of the previous two decades of experience in Europe; no less important is its capacity to grip the reader with new psychological insights. Margaret Canovan calls it a 'work of art'.[10]

One such insight is Arendt's highly plausible explanation of the staggering phenomenon of the 'fading' of post-war Nazis into respectable society.

> It is in the moment of defeat that the inherent weakness of totalitarian propaganda becomes visible. Without the force of the movement, its members cease at once to believe in the dogmas for which yesterday they were prepared to sacrifice their lives. The moment the movement, that is the fictitious world which sheltered them, is destroyed, the masses revert to their old status of isolated individuals who either happily accept a new function in a changed world or sink back into their old desperate superfluousness. The members of totalitarian movements, utterly fanatical as long as the movement exists, will not follow the example of religious fanatics and die the death of robots . . .
>
> The experience of the Allies who vainly tried to locate one self-confessed and convinced Nazi among the German people, 90 per cent of whom probably had been sincere sympathizers at one time or another, is not to be taken as a sign of human weakness or gross opportunism. Nazism as an ideology had been so fully 'realized' that its content ceased to exist as an independent set of doctrines, lost its intellectual existence, so to speak; destruction of the reality therefore left almost nothing behind, least of all the fanaticism of the believers.[11]

Phenomenologically satisfying though this type of analysis may be, Arendt warns against assuming its intellectual coherence. Disclaimers are studded through the work, like the failure to understand the translation of racist doctrine into racist murder (she says 'there is an abyss between the men of brilliant and facile conception,' from Gobineau to the eugenicists, and 'the men of brutal deeds and active bestiality which no intellectual explanation is able to bridge').[12] Similarly, she warns against the 'liberal rationalization' of all the steps towards terror and the ultimate laboratory of the concentration camp: 'In each of one of us there lurks such a liberal, wheedling us with the voice of common sense. The road to totalitarian domination leads through many intermediate stages for which we can find numerous analogues and precedents.'[13]

Finally, there is a stark confrontation with what she calls here for the first time, echoing Kant, 'radical evil'. Arendt directly equates the possible victory of the concentration-camp system with the use of the hydrogen bomb: 'Here, there are neither political nor historical nor simply moral standards but at the most, the realization that something seems to be involved in modern politics that actually should never have been involved in politics as we used to understand it.'[14]

In the face of this and the recognition that 'when the impossible was made the possible it became the unpunishable,' it is hard to avoid the conclusion that Arendt's implicit goal in *The Origins of Totalitarianism*, the development of 'discerning judgement', had failed: 'we actually have nothing to fall back on in order to understand a phenomenon that nevertheless confronts us with its overpowering reality and breaks down all standards we know.'[15] In these circumstances assigning responsibility and reaching judgements appears almost impossible. Nevertheless, in a series of statements which pre-dated and followed *The Origins of Totalitarianism*, Arendt made her own detailed contribution to investigations into the case of Germany.

Guilt and Responsibility

Arendt set out her more abstract ideas about collective responsibility in two articles separated by almost twenty years. The first, 'Organized Guilt and Universal Responsibility', initially published in *Jewish Frontier* in 1945, was written when German defeat was inevitable but had not yet happened. The second, 'Personal Responsibility under Dictatorship', based on a talk broadcast on American and British radio in 1964, was throughout informed by the Eichmann trial.

'Organized Guilt' begins with the problems the Allies had set themselves of defining and punishing war criminals. In particular, the wartime propaganda which had elided the concepts of 'German' and 'Nazi' would, in her view, make both processes impossible. What is more, she saw a dreadful complicity of the Nazis themselves in creating this dilemma: 'As long as the Nazis expected victory, their terror organizations were strictly isolated from the people and, in time of war, from the army . . . It was only their defeats which forced the Nazis to abandon this concept and pretend to return to old nationalist slogans.'[16] Ironically, this meant that the only secure way to identify an anti-Nazi 'is when the Nazis have hanged him'.

Thus the concept of collective guilt, and all of its popular perversions of the time (such as the slogan that 'the only good German is a dead German'), depends upon an 'inverted version of Nazi racial theory'. Nazi totalitarianism, which 'has made the existence of each individual in Germany depend either upon committing crimes or on complicity in crimes', is matched by a fatal lack of discrimination in external judgement.[17] For Arendt, these appalling facts lead to a vital distinction between guilt and responsibility: 'guilt implies a consciousness of guilt, and punishment evidence that the criminal is a responsible person.'[18] The Nazis and other Germans had created this dilemma in at least two ways. The latter had either been sympathetic to or had at least tolerated Hitler's rise to power. 'Yet these people, who were co-responsible for Hitler's crimes in a broader sense, did not incur any guilt in a stricter sense. They, who were the Nazis' first accomplices and their best aides, truly did not know what they were doing nor with whom they were dealing.'[19] The former (the Nazis), exemplified here particularly by Himmler, had in their mobilization of the 'family man', and the privatization of conscience, achieved a devastating variety of moral *Gleichshaltung*: 'for the sake of his pension, his life insurance, the security of his wife and children, such a man was to sacrifice his beliefs, his honour, and his human dignity.'[20] This elevation of the private over the public allowed the individual to be 'fully exempted from responsibility for his acts'.

One conclusion from this analysis is a kind of despair for the process of justice and the possibility of punishment.

> Just as there is no political solution within human capacity for the crime of administrative mass murder, so the human need for justice can find no satisfactory reply to the total mobilization of a people for that purpose. Where all are guilty, nobody in the last analysis can be judged.

Even the victims are stained by the consequences. Commenting on Jewish refugees and the targets of the Gestapo who had succeeded in escaping, Arendt finds them in the forefront of the reverse ideology. In a footnote which presages some of the views which Jewish readers later found so offensive in *Eichmann in Jerusalem*, she discusses their avoidance of such guilt through timing and 'not through their own merit':

> Because they know this and because their horror at what might have been still haunts them, they often introduce into discussion of this kind that insufferable tone of self-righteousness which frequently and particularly among Jews

can turn into the vulgar obverse of Nazi doctrines; and in fact already has.[21]

What potentially redeems the situation (and we must remember the wartime circumstances in which the essay was written in order to recognize how important such redemption was to Arendt) is 'shame' at the events which have unfolded – not only shame expressed by Germans, but the 'elemental' shame which Arendt feels as a human being – and its political consequences. The suppression of 'civic virtue' by 'private calculation' of participating and acquiescing Germans may have been encouraged by a native political tradition ('hardly another culture of Occidental Culture was so little imbued with the classic virtues of civic behaviour'), but it also inspires an obligation on the part of a wider humanity to recognize its causes and consequences.[22]

> For the idea of humanity, when purged of all sentimentality, has the very serious consequence that in one form or another men must assume responsibility for all crimes committed by men and that all nations share the onus of evil committed by all others. Shame at being a human being is the purely individual and still non-political expression of this insight.[23]

Collective responsibility has become universal responsibility.

The political corollary should be not a hypocritical leap to unsustainable general judgement of German national character ('God be thanked, I am not like that'), but a realization 'of what man is capable' ('the precondition of any modern political theory'). Persons capable of judging in this way 'will not serve very well as functionaries of vengeance'; they can, however, be relied upon to fight 'fearlessly, uncompromisingly, everywhere against the incalculable evil that men are capable of bringing about'.[24]

'Personal Responsibility under Dictatorship', perhaps freed of the more exhortatory obligations of the wartime context of 'Organized Guilt', starts its analysis from a similar point but develops it much further. Arendt begins emphatically by repudiating terms such as 'collective guilt or collective innocence'; she says, 'these terms make sense only if applied to individuals.' She then turns to the arguments that have complicated this assertion, and which surfaced in the Eichmann trial. The first is that of the 'cog-theory' whereby personal responsibility is displaced by the individual's position in a large administrative system ('If I had not done it somebody else could and would').[25] This the Israeli court had rightly and effectively dismissed, 'because even a functionary is still a human being, and it is in this capacity that he stands trial'.

However, it leads on to a further problem. In the social and political conditions discussed in 'Organized Guilt', only total withdrawal would have ensured non-implication. In these circumstances an additional argument can be developed about the 'lesser evil', which states that those who withdrew lost their chance to mitigate the effects of the machine and thought only of their own personal salvation. Looking later in the article at functionaries who, to a man, claimed never to have been convinced adherents, now 'every single one of them, wherever he stood and whatever he did, claims that those who, under one pretext or another, had returned into private life had chosen the easy, the irresponsible way out.' The inescapable weakness of this argument is that, in Arendt's words, 'those who choose the lesser evil forget quickly that they chose evil.'[26]

This is, of course, a context in which moral 'judgement'

is almost impossible. Acceptance of lesser evils started a process 'until a stage was reached where nothing worse could happen'. In the course of this process the participants lost all their secure moral reference points.

In the face of this morally anomic world Arendt shifts from moral to legal standards 'because these are generally better defined'. She discusses carefully, separately, and then dismisses two arguments about the personal responsibility of war criminals. The first, that they are carrying out 'acts of state' which would technically remove the consequence from legal jurisdiction, is rejected because of the failure to demonstrate the 'necessity' of the 'crime' to the survival of the state: 'What neither the political reason-of-state theory nor the legal concept of acts of state foresaw was the complete reversal of legality; in the case of the Hitler regime there was hardly an act of state which according to moral standards was not criminal.' Similarly, the argument from 'superior orders' collapses as the assumption that the 'receiver of orders can be expected to recognize the criminal nature of a particular order' was inapplicable in these circumstances.

The judges in post-war trials (in Jerusalem and elsewhere) failed because they presupposed the capacity of the individuals involved to judge themselves. They assumed that there existed 'an independent human faculty, unsupported by law and public opinion, that judges anew in full spontaneity every deed and intent whenever the occasion arises'. In the condition of a 'gruesomely novel *order*' such as Nazi Germany, this was not a reasonable presupposition.[27]

From here Arendt exposes two further fallacies: that the critical actions were those of a limited 'gang of criminals' (she had disposed of this in 'Organized Guilt') and that they reflected an outbreak of modern nihilism (which is not far from her previous formulation). Instead of the earlier political prescription, she insists on drawing the question back into its own legal framework. 'Genocide' and 'extermination of whole peoples' has happened before, for example in colonization. Here the obscenity was that the command took effect within 'the frame of a legal order', and she cites the opinion of Eichmann's lawyer that extermination of the Jews had been a 'medical matter'.

Arendt then directs our attention to those who did not collaborate, and draws a philosophical rather than a political conclusion.

> The non-participants, called irresponsible by the majority, were the only ones who dared to judge by themselves, and they were capable of doing so not because they disposed of a better system of values or because the old standards of right and wrong were still firmly planted in their mind and conscience but, I would suggest, because their conscience did not function in this, as it were automatic way – as though we dispose of a set of learned or innate rules which we then apply to the particular case as it arises, so that every new experience or situation is already prejudged and we need only act out whatever we learned or possessed beforehand. Their criterion, I think, was a different one: they asked themselves to what an extent they would still be able to live with themselves after having committed certain deeds; and they decided that it would be better to do nothing not because the world would then be changed for the better, but because only on this condition could they go on living with themselves.

The consequences were stark. 'Hence they also chose to die when they were forced to participate.'

Arendt emphasizes that these individuals were not necessarily well-educated or philosophically expressive. 'The presupposition for this kind of judging is not a highly developed intelligence or sophistication in matters, but merely the habit of living together explicitly with oneself, that is, of being engaged in that silent dialogue between me and myself which since Socrates and Plato we usually call thinking.' Those who are prepared to think are the 'doubters and sceptics' who are 'used to examin(ing) things and to mak(ing) up their own minds'.

An argument earlier in the essay would have also charged them with irresponsibility, an accusation Arendt sets aside because political responsibility implies political power, or the ability to change objective circumstances. Since circumstances were not susceptible to change she suggests, finally, that the category of 'obedience' appealed to by so many as a virtue, or at least as an excuse, is inappropriate. Genuine political 'support' of a 'leader' who is 'never more than the first among his peers' is different. The non-participants refused to support in precisely the same way as other modern exponents of non-violent resistance. 'The reason why we can hold these new criminals, who never committed a crime out of their own initiative nevertheless responsible for what they did is that there is no such thing as obedience in political and moral matters.'[28]

For her, later, the Eichmann case, properly read, confirmed this philosophical conclusion.

Jaspers and The Question of German Guilt

Arendt's concern about the concept and implications of collective guilt was shared with Jaspers, although she had reservations about the spiritual rather than political tone with which he expressed them. In *The Question of German Guilt* (1947), the English-language edition of which she arranged, he speaks directly to students under the post-war occupation government urging them to recognize and overcome their political and moral situation: 'such a historical self-analysis of our German being is at the same time an ethical self-examination.'[29]

Jaspers' taxonomy of types of guilt is broader than Arendt's, but his conclusion is similar. He distinguishes between *criminal* guilt violating 'unequivocal laws', *political* guilt ('everybody is co-responsible for the way he is governed'), *moral* guilt where 'jurisdiction rests with my conscience', and *metaphysical* guilt, based on the 'solidarity among men as human beings that makes each co-responsible for every wrong and every injustice in the world, especially for crimes committed in his presence or with his knowledge'.[30] However, 'it is nonsensical . . . to charge a whole people with a crime. The criminal is always only an individual . . . Thus there can be no collective guilt of a people or group within a people – except for political liability.'[31]

Jaspers also offers a fuller account of the choices made by individual Germans manifested in their varieties of co-responsibility ('disguise', 'false consciousness', 'running with the pack' etc.) and of their excuses (the so-called 'terrorist state', 'history', 'geography' and 'world-historical' malaise).[32]

His message for this domestic audience about the consequence of German guilt is more immediate, and, at least indirectly, casts doubt upon Arendt's appeal to universal responsibility. All Germans share the 'political liability', some are directly liable for crimes committed, most need 'moral self-analysis', and every German 'capable of thinking' will 'transform his approach to the world'. The outcome is a rejection, for these purposes, of the concept of original sin, and a proposal for national purification or 'making amends'.³³ For Jaspers the unmastered past is a German problem.

The same focus on national responsibility and expiation continued to haunt Jaspers. In 1965 he was forced to return to it in the precise political context of whether the statute of limitations on Nazi murders should be extended by the parliament of the Federal Republic. In a dialogue with the editor of *Der Spiegel*, translated and published in *Commentary*, he goes back to the questions of political will and political liability. Consistently urged by Rudolf Augstein to make international and historical comparisons, he refuses to be tempted. Instead he redirects the dialogue to German responsibility for the actions and consequences of a 'criminal state'. He also develops a concept, similar to Arendt's charge against Eichmann, of a 'crime against mankind' and its unique horror when compared with other war crimes. 'All who have grasped this (Hannah Arendt first of all) today declare with express conviction: no man has the right to judge that a people should not exist.'³⁴

Like Arendt on the Eichmann trial (see Chapter Five), he also regrets the deficiencies of international law and, as in 1945, fears local (i.e., national) backsliding. For him, the prime need is to align with a western moral consensus, about which (from the transatlantic perspective) Arendt was more inclined to be pessimistic.

> If the Germans don't stand up as men and women who really have the will to found a new state, after the fearful things they did or suffered to be done – then it is almost cause for despair . . . If we do not get in step with the harmony that today can be felt to exist from America to all the

European countries, then we will yet again isolate ourselves morally.[35]

Other judgements – Men in Dark Times

Closer to home Arendt's judgements were less convincing than in the case of Eichmann. Not only were Heidegger and Jaspers both Arendt's teachers, but the former had been her lover and the latter was the individual whose approval she perhaps most desired (and whose criticism she most feared in her later life). In the course of World War II they took dramatically different routes: Heidegger as a now well-exposed collaborator, indeed enthusiast for Nazism (from which his career benefited spectacularly); Jaspers (whose wife was Jewish) as a principled objector and analyst of German responsibility for the Holocaust. If ever there was a case for Arendt to exercise retrospective judgement on an individual basis this seems it. Arendt's actions are interesting and puzzling: she praised Jaspers generously, and she exonerated Heidegger. In fact, she applied to each different standards, and a different model of what the philosopher should be.

In an encomium, 'Heidegger at Eighty', published in the *New York Review of Books* in 1971, Arendt stressed Heidegger's reputation among philosophers and students of philosophy, and his embodiment of the philosophical ideas of stillness and solitude (this is one of the rare examples of her elevation of Plato over Aristotle). Against this background his political activities are seen as an aberration, and the details relegated to a footnote. In the main text she refers to the issue obliquely – 'Now we all know that Heidegger, too, once succumbed to the temptation to change his "residence" and to get involved in the world of human affairs.' The footnote to this passage points to his misunderstanding of the message of Nazism, which had nothing to do with the 'encounter between global technology and modern men', as he claimed in his *Introduction to Metaphysics*: 'Heidegger like so many other German intellectuals, Nazis and anti-Nazis, of his generation never read *Mein Kampf*'.

From here the exoneration proceeds apace. First, there is Heidegger's youth and impressionability: 'He was still young enough to learn from the first shock of the collision, which after ten hectic months thirty-seven years ago drove him back to his residence, and to settle in his thinking what he had experienced.' Then there is the argument from precedent:

> We who wish to honour the thinkers, even if our own residence lies in the midst of the world, can hardly help finding it striking and perhaps exasperating that Plato and Heidegger, when they entered into human affairs, turned to tyrants and Führers . . . For the attraction to the tyrannical can be demonstrated in many of the great thinkers (Kant is the great exception).[36]

Jaspers, who for Arendt was the twentieth century's incarnation of Kant, especially in his hopes for world citizenship, proved to be a shining knight in comparison to Heidegger (who had the gall after the war to offer himself to the occupying forces as a tutor in the denazification programme). However, she relies as much on a structural as on a personal estimate of his work.

In the introduction to her collection of essays, *Men in Dark Times*, Arendt repeats her explanation of Heidegger's inadequacy in the public realm.

> There is no escape, according to Heidegger, from the 'incomprehensible triviality' of this common everyday world

except by withdrawal from it to the solitude which philosophers since Parmenides and Plato have opposed to the political realm.[37]

Later in the book she reprints a translation of her *laudatio* for Jaspers on the occasion of his award of the German Book Trade's Peace Prize in 1958, including particular praise for his acceptance of the public realm: 'to say in public what many know in the seclusion of privacy is not superfluous. The very fact that something is being heard by all confers upon it an illuminating power that confirms its real existence.'[38]

In three key works – *Man in the Modern Age*, *The Question of German Guilt*, and *The Atom Bomb and the Future of Man* – Jaspers is shown to have 'intervened directly in political questions of the day'. The difference is not merely one of personality (although it is hard to see Heidegger as an embodiment of *humanitas* in the same way) or temperament. Jaspers is praised for doing precisely what Heidegger should not have done. In another essay in the same collection, otherwise respectfully critical of Jaspers' adaption of Kant's ideal of world citizenship, his strength is seen as Heidegger's imputed weakness:

> Jaspers is, as far as I know, the first and only philosopher who has ever protested against solitude, to whom solitude has appeared 'pernicious' and who has dared to question 'all thoughts, all experiences, all talents' under this aspect: 'what do they signify for communication? Are they such that they may help or such that they will prevent communication? Do they seduce to solitude or arouse to communication?'[39]

In this case the harsh conclusion has to be that Arendt avoided, for personal reasons, the application of her own standards of judgement.

Other individual portraits Arendt collected in *Men in Dark Times*, which is comprised of essays written between 1955 and 1968. Each subject was for her an example of heroism through the preservation of 'a minimum of humanity in the world grown inhuman'. The concept of 'dark times', borrowed from Brecht, itself relies on the loss of proper politics and the temptation to inner emigration that Arendt found so disastrous among many of her German contemporaries. In dark times 'the public realm has been obscured and the world become[s] so dubious that people have ceased to ask any more of politics than that it show due consideration for their vital interests and personal liberty.'[40]

Her other characters are all, with the exception of the poet Gotthold Lessing, from the 'first half of the twentieth century with its political catastrophes, its moral disasters, and its astonishing development of the arts and sciences'.[41] Each is a separate, individual story of heroism, from the socialist Rosa Luxemburg, and the contemporary story-tellers Isak Dinesen and Randall Jarrell, to Pope John XXIII (Cardinal Roncalli) whose outspokenness on behalf of European Jews is seen as giving moral meaning to his ministry.[42]

Each subject demonstrates at least one of Arendt's personal set of heroic qualities. Luck, good and bad, played a significant part in their fates, especially that of Walter Benjamin who committed suicide when his escape-route to Spain was suddenly closed for a single night. 'Only on that particular day was the catastrophe possible.'[43] However, more significant in each story is the characters' qualities of compassion or fellow-feeling, and their resistance to simplistic or authoritarian ideology. The poet Hermann Broch, for example, saw all relationships governed by an ethical imperative to 'helpfulness', while the political scientist Waldemar Gurian's central insight, like that of the great Russian writers, was 'into the true quality of humiliation and . . . passion for the down trodden'.[44] Brecht's 'doctrinaire and often ludicrous adherence to the Communist ideology', is similarly deplored, and although Arendt took his side when the American philosopher Sidney Hook accused him of justifying the purges ordered by Stalin, it finally emerged for Arendt in this morally mistaken view that 'those who, compelled by passion, set out to change the world cannot afford to be good.'[45]

What Brecht, and others Arendt admired, did possess was the poet's or *Dichter's* intuition and ability to communicate. This could overcome (at least for Brecht) the poet's tendency to be unreliable as a citizen and to misbehave; another example for Arendt is Ezra Pound whose support for fascism scarcely impaired his expressive power as a poet.[46] At its best, poetry (the example here is Lessing's) has the 'power of illumination' and is a kind of 'action'. An artist, like the story-teller (the examples here are Dinesen and Jarrell), is chiefly important for his 'effect upon the spectator, who as it were represents the world, or rather that worldly space which has come into being between the artist or writer and his fellow man as a world common to them'.[47] Dinesen, the Danish author, whose *Gothic Tales* and writings about her life in Africa with the explorer Denys Finch-Hatton have recently undergone a revival, demonstrated for Arendt the great saving power and truthfulness of reflection, 'recollection' and story-telling. 'Story-telling reveals meaning without committing the error of defining it . . . it brings about consent and reconciliation with things as they really are, and . . . we may trust it to contain eventually by implication that last word which we expect from the "day of judgement".'[48]

Methodologically, what this and the character sketches lead us towards is the retrospective essence of judgement and the primacy of history. Borrowing Benjamin's notion of the 'angel of history', Arendt too confirms the supremacy of the backward perspective over the futuristic, progressive illusions of grand dialectical schemes. 'The "angel of history" . . . does not dialectically move forward into the future, but has his face "turned towards the past". "Where a chain of events appears to *us*, *he* sees one single catastrophe which keeps piling wreckage upon wreckage and hurls it in front of his feet." '[49]

What several of Arendt's subjects have in common is a particular fate in the twentieth-century history of Germany (several also share the insight into the political basis of Zionism discussed in Chapter Four). In her essay on Lessing (1959) she makes a comment on the unmasterable past that comes close to summing up the clear-eyed vision found in the best of men in dark times. Discussing contemporary Germans' 'profound awkwardness' in talking about their immediate past she sets out some preliminary ideas on how this is to be overcome.

> How difficult it must be to find a reasonable attitude is perhaps more clearly expressed by the cliché that the past is still 'unmastered' and in the conviction held particularly by men of good will that the first thing to be done is to set about 'mastering' it. Perhaps that cannot be done with any past, but certainly not with the past of Hitler Germany. The best that can be done is to know precisely what it was, and to endure this knowledge, and then to wait and see what comes of knowing and enduring.[50]

Reports from Germany

In the immediate aftermath of the war Arendt developed a role as an 'expert' on the German problem, writing articles and reviews and visiting the defeated country in 1949. Her expertise was also confirmed by some practical assignments for Jewish Cultural Reconstruction, of which she became a director in 1948, and her position as a columnist on the German emigré newspaper *Aufbau*. Together these roles enabled Arendt to test theories she was developing for *The Origins of Totalitarianism*, to flesh out some of her ideas about judgement and responsibility, and to attempt to influence American views of the evolving political situation in Europe.

Much of her analysis was unrelentingly pessimistic. The reversion of German society to its 'unpolitical' normality reinforced what she called in October 1950 'a deep-rooted, stubborn, and at times vicious refusal to come to terms with what really happened'. The occupying powers had failed to achieve much through denazification, and the prospects for moral revival in their policies of free enterprise and federalism were equally gloomy. 'In less than six years Germany laid waste the moral structure of western society . . . But nowhere is this nightmare of destruction less felt and talked about than in Germany itself.' Writing a 'report from Germany' for readers of *Commentary*, Arendt concluded 'totalitarianism kills the roots.'[51]

In 1965 the social scientist Ralf Dahrendorf caused uproar in German intellectual circles by concluding his *Society and Democracy in Germany* with an 'excursus' on the question 'how was Auschwitz possible?' Much of his exposition is indistinguishable from Arendt's earlier thought, in particular the discovery of the shallowness and brittleness of German cultural life in the face of Nazism: 'the inhumanity of letting the weak and those in need of care suffer, coupled with empty humanistic talk, is the recognizable beginning of a chain that does not exclude the mass murder of defenceless people.'[52] The qualities of *Innigkeit* ('inwardness') which she so valued in German poetry had had corrosive and then fatal effects on German political life.[53]

For Arendt there was a macabre humour in the readiness of German intellectuals to come to the aid of the party and their indifferent success. The Nazis did not 'use' the ideas that were the cultural flowers of German civilization; they had had their own ideas and merely needed 'techniques and technicians'. 'That not one of the first-rate German scholars ever attained to a position of influence is a fact, but this fact does not mean that they did not try to.'[54]

One theme in Arendt's first-hand accounts, then, was an elaboration of the 'crime against humanity' and the potential generalization of the fate of the Jewish people. Post-war attempts to come to terms with this crime almost always failed. Reverse propaganda was inherently flawed. Reviewing *The Black Book*, a compilation of evidence about the Holocaust by the World Jewish Congress, Arendt commented that the authors 'lack the power to make the whole German nation *look* as guilty as the Nazis made the Jews look'.[55]

The 'Historikerstreit'

The problems posed by Arendt and Jaspers have, of course, not gone away, nor have they progressed much in terms of the scope and sophistication of the solutions proposed. They resurfaced internationally with the further extension of the statute of limitations on Nazi war crimes in 1979, and more recently with the visit of President Reagan to a cemetery including the graves of SS officers (Bitburg) in 1985. They also lay behind the resignation of the President of the West German Parliament, Phillip Jenniger, after a speech on the fiftieth anniversary of the *Reichkristallnacht* in which he tried to explain some of the circumstances of the national pogrom against the Jews in 1938. In public discourse a continuing point of reference is the 'struggle of the historians' ('Historikerstreit'), which for the last five years at least has brought the ideas and activities of West German political historians into the public arena. In 1990–1 they were given added poignancy in the headlong rush to reunification of the two post-war Germanies.

The issues in the 'Historikerstreit' are philosophically simple but politically complex. On the one hand, a 'conservative tendency' led by Ernst Nolte urges a revision of the received view of the uniqueness of the Holocaust, pointing to the Russian responsibility for the Gulag, a German conviction that the nation was defending itself against a comparable 'Asiatic deed', and the identification internationally of the Jews as enemies of the Hitler state.

This is, however, a revisionist conservatism. Spokesmen for the deeper continuities of German political history have relied precisely on the identification of the Holocaust as an aberration. Other more moderate voices on the right wing of the argument such as Michael Stürmer and the late Andreas Hillgruber, are concerned to overcome the 'pathological' preoccupation with the execution of the Final Solution and to revive the possibility of a healthy German patriotism. In ideological and practical terms they are close to the CDU/CSU government of Chancellor Kohl. Their values are defined more in terms of 'normalizing' the past than the efforts at 'relativization' preached by Nolte, and they associate an obsession with the Holocaust with the decadence and cultural breakdown of the 1960s. In Stürmer's words:

> The cultural policy of the '60s sowed the wind and today we are reaping the tempest. If we do not succeed in agreeing on an elementary cultural curriculum, with which to prepare the way for continuity and consensus in the country and to find once more the measure and mode of patriotism, then it may well be that the Federal Republic of Germany has the best part of its history behind it.[56]

In international terms both Nolte and his more moderate allies wished to find a moral platform from which to criticize the Western alliance, particularly when it was in danger of underestimating the threat of Eastern bloc communism.

For the left, and in particular for the social theorist Jürgen Habermas, this is dangerous political as well as moral rubbish. The identity of a democratic Federal Republic rests precisely on an acceptance of responsibility for the outrageous crimes committed by the pre-war and wartime German state. This is a precondition for modern, pluralist constitutionalism, and an identification of secure political values. In terms very similar to those of Jaspers he declares that:

> The only patriotism that will not alienate us from the West is constitutional patriotism. Unfortunately, a tie to universal constitutional principles that is based upon conviction has only been possible in Germany since and because of, Auschwitz. Anyone who wants to drive the blush of shame over the deed from our cheeks by using meaningless phrases like 'obsession with guilt', anyone who wants to call

Germans back to a conventional kind of identity, destroys
the only reliable basis of our tie to the West.[57]

On the political map this locates Habermas close to the SPD opposition. Further to the left Marxists and Greens question the authenticity of the post-war constitution itself. Like the right they point instead to German political continuities, but their continuities are of authoritarianism achieving a final perversion in the Nazi years, rather than of national leadership and pride. Methodologically, they have their own champions in a German version of the *History Workshop* movement, inspired by the late Martin Broszat and the Institute for Contemporary History.

There is a variety of elements at play here: continuity versus discontinuity in German history; national identity versus western pluralism; shame versus displacement of responsibility; consciousness of the uniqueness of a crime against humanity versus a search for the comfort of precedent or analogy; all of which are central to the efforts of Arendt and Jaspers to analyse and deal with guilt and responsibility.

PART II

Israel:

THE POLITICAL NECESSITY
OF ZIONISM

CHAPTER FOUR

Arendt and Zionism

For all of her administrative and publicity work for Zionist organizations, and her contribution to heated debates such as that about the creation of a Jewish army in the early 1940s, Hannah Arendt was not a passionate Zionist. Like many moderate Jewish intellectuals, she saw the state of Israel as a political necessity rather than the realization of a prophecy.

History

Arendt's understanding of anti-Semitism, and of Zionism as a reaction to it, was sophisticated and complex, but permanently connected to a simple historical thesis about the Jewish role in European history, set out most fully in *The Origins of Totalitarianism*. 'Modern anti-Semitism grew in proportion as traditional nationalism declined, and reached its climax at the exact moment when the European system of nation-states and its precarious balance of power crashed.'[1]

Arendt's thesis ties the fate of the Jewish people together with that of the modern state through a web of economic and social services. Jewish money financed the nineteenth-century states' bureaucracy and infrastructure, and provided a necessary degree of internationalism through diplomacy and financial services as nationalism flourished. In these circumstances anti-

Semitism was containable, largely as a lower middle-class campaign against banking capital as well as in some intermittent claims of an alternative supranationalism (pan-Germanism, for example). Before World War I, then, the Jews were disproportionately deluded by the 'Golden Age of Security'. Anti-Semitic episodes like the trial and conviction of the Jewish Officer Dreyfus in France in 1894 were merely a 'huge dress rehearsal' for what was to come.

Special problems arose for Jews because of their confusion of political and social equality. 'Political anti-Semitism developed because the Jews were a separate body, while social discrimination arose because of the growing equality of Jews with all other groups.'[2] These were the circumstances in which Rahel Varnhagen's choice of 'pariah' or 'parvenu' roles (a concept here attributed to Karl Kraus) became vital. A parvenu such as Disraeli 'played his part so well that he was convinced by his own make-believe'.[3]

After the catastrophe of World War I such self-deception became impossible to sustain. With the development of mob anti-Semitism and scapegoating the truth was out. Assimilation had never been a permanent solution. Judaism as a 'crime' which could be 'cleansed' by conversion was overwhelmed by the 'vice' of Jewishness, from which there is no escape. This was the context of the emergence of Zionism as a counter-ideology. 'The only visible result (of the Dreyfus affair) was that it gave birth to the Zionist movement... the only political answer Jews have ever found to anti-Semitism.'[4]

Zionism: theory and practice

The chief philosophical architect of Zionism was Theodore Herzl (1860 – 1904), whose nineteenth-century formulations

Arendt found to be fatally flawed in the new conditions of the twentieth century. Herzl, the founder of the World Zionist Organization in 1897, had seen anti-Semitism as a rational, enduring (or 'eternal') reaction of European societies to the existence of the Jewish people of the diaspora. With the aid of 'honest anti-Semites' it should thus be possible to win the argument and the political resources to recreate the Jewish homeland and return the people to it. For Arendt this view was static, perilously unresponsive to historical reality, and permitted only a single, high-diplomatic solution to the problem. In her influential article of 1945, 'Zionism Reconsidered', she characterizes it as 'selling out at the first moment to the powers-that-be'.[5]

Even more problematic than the flaws in Herzl's initial analysis was its staying-power. Arendt shows how his aims, especially of a political guarantee or 'charter', signifying agreement of the Great Powers to the establishment of Palestine as a Jewish home, became converted into the 'practical Zionism' (later termed 'general Zionism') of Chaim Weizmann (1874–1952), elected the first President of Israel in 1949. In this transformation the seeds of further conflict were sown as the western intellectual inheritors of Herzl's ideology found it put into practice by the mass of eastern, poorer, less well-educated Jews who constituted the bulk of inter-war Jewish immigration into Palestine.[6]

For Arendt these immigrants, who inspired experimental patterns of social settlement like the kibbutz, were continuing the ideals of a suppressed tradition in western Zionist thought and were the true inheritors of Jewish mystical and separatist traditions. Her Zionist hero was the French socialist Bernard Lazare (1865–1903), whose essays she published in New York, as one of her first projects for Schocken Books, under the title

Job's Dungheap: Essays on Jewish Nationalism and Social Revolution (1948). Lazare, who came from an assimilated Sephardic family, published a two-volume analysis of anti-Semitism in 1894 in which he saw a solution, directly opposing Herzl's, in the possibility of the withering away of the nation-state. Later, he was a counsel to the Dreyfus family, and at the end of the affair refused, unlike his client, to accept a presidential pardon. In 1899 he founded *Le Flambeau*, a short-lived 'organ of Zionist and social Judaism'. He died at the age of thirty-eight, isolated within the Jewish community, but his legacy represented for Arendt a significant road not taken.[7]

In Paris and in New York Arendt had the chance to put her own ideas about 'political Zionism' into practice. From 1935 until January 1939, when the operation was taken over for security reasons by the London branch of WIZO (the Women's International Zionist Organization), Arendt ran the Paris base of Youth Aliyah, a scheme for preparing and assisting young Jewish refugees in their relocation to Palestine. In 1935 she accompanied one of the groups on her last visit to Israel before she returned in 1961 for the Eichmann trial. She also engaged Chanon Klenbort, the Polish Jewish writer who married her childhood friend Lotte Sempel, to teach her Hebrew.[8]

Simultaneously, she was involved in monitoring right-wing anti-Semitism (with special attention to the *Action Française*) and in trying to organize a legal defence for two Jewish assassins of Nazi leaders: David Frankfurter in February 1936, and Hermann Grynzpan (whose father later gave evidence in the Eichmann trial) in November 1938.

As Elisabeth Young-Bruehl points out, a leitmotiv of Arendt's activities at this stage was the argument against *T'schuwah*, the concept of 'return' or 'return to the ghetto', as it could so easily become in these circumstances. Her concern was for the fate of European Jewry, which could not be wholly secured by opportunities in Israel. A 'withdrawal from the European cultural community' could not be the right response.[9]

Within two years, of course, Arendt and her family had to withdraw themselves, physically, to New York. Here, throughout the 1940s she took part in key debates about the Zionist role in the conduct of the war and its outcomes, including the nature of the settlement in Palestine. From late 1941 until 1944 she wrote a regular column for the emigré newspaper *Aufbau* (loosely translated as 'construction' or 'building'). Her contributions continued more intermittently up to 1963.

Through *Aufbau* she became most noteworthy for her championship of the idea of a Jewish army, which was rejected as a practical option by the British as early as October 1941 on security grounds. Arendt continued the campaign even after its most prominent American sponsor, Ben Hecht's Committee for a Jewish Army, was exposed as a front for the revisionist (extreme nationalist) wing of the Zionist movement. She even briefly sponsored an alternative group – the Young Jewish Group – to carry the campaign forward. In this, as in everything else, she was supported by Blücher, one of whose youthful political memberships had been of a Zionist group.[10]

Arendt's concept of the Jewish army was always more broadly based than Hecht's. She saw the idea as a rallying of the diaspora rather than a liberation of the homeland, and was particularly conscious, as she simultaneously worked on her historical studies of World War I, of the need for a Jewish presence in the peace settlement at the end of World War II.[11] By the mid-1940s any such hope for the future influence of European Jewry was lost, as Arendt subsequently acknowledged in *The Origins of Totalitarianism*. The news from Europe was devastating for Arendt and Blücher. It was at this stage that she wrote the poem 'Park on the Hudson', which includes the phrase 'the burden of time' used for the title of the first British edition of *The Origins of Totalitarianism*.

> Children playing, mothers calling them.
> Eternity is almost here.
> A loving couple passes by
> Bearing the burden of time.[12]

There was, however, a major task of record and rescue to be accomplished, and from 1944 she took the job of research director for the Conference on Jewish Relations (later the Conference on Jewish Social Studies). In this capacity she oversaw the Herculean task of cataloguing Jewish cultural and religious artefacts and began the process that led to the post-war recovery, from Nazi *caches* as well as from the chaos and confusion resulting from the war, of a mass of Hebrew treasures. From 1948 until 1952 she was the executive director of Jewish Cultural Reconstruction, a project which she led in the field for six months in 1949–50. Young-Bruehl lists the achievement of the project as the recovery of '1.5 million volumes of Hebraica and Judaica, thousands of ceremonial and artistic objects, and over a thousand scrolls of law'.[13]

Palestine: state or homeland

Throughout the 1940s Arendt developed her theoretical commitment to Zionism through commentary, sometimes minutely partisan, on the struggle for Palestine and the early years of the state of Israel. In the maelstrom of Palestinian domestic and exile politics, her position was difficult to identify with any one party or group. For example, she covered the 1942 Biltmore conference of international Zionists for *Aufbau* and found fault both with Weizmann's overtures to the British occupiers and David Ben-Gurion's passionate call for a 'Jewish Palestine' involving the forcible relocation of Arab populations. Subsequent formulations like the call of Judah Magnes (the first President of the Hebrew University and founder of the *Ikhud* ('Unity') party in August 1942) for a bi-national Palestine as part of an Arab Federation found no more favour.[14]

Arendt's own position was subtle, subject to change, and without any real hope of being politically persuasive. As she argued in a series of articles in the late 1940s – from 'Zionism Reconsidered' (first published in the *Menorah Journal*, August 1945), to 'To Save the Jewish Homeland: There is Still Time' (in *Commentary*, May 1948) and 'Peace and Armistice in the New East' (*Review of Politics*, January 1950) – the various brands of Zionism were dangerously partial and held no real prospect of lasting peace and prosperity: 'a Jewish state can only be erected as the price of the Jewish homeland.'[15] If she was close to any one party it was *Brith Shalom*, the group of intellectuals around Magnes and Martin Buber who opposed the separate Israeli state.[16] For this she paid the price of alienation from a growing wedge of American Jewish opinion, being branded a 'collaborationist' by one contributor to the *Jewish Frontier*.[17]

As Young-Bruehl and others have pointed out, Arendt's preference would have been for the transplantation of the founding achievement of the American republic, with its implications of federal co-operation, to the Middle East. At one stage she even saw the possibility of Palestine developing best within the British Commonwealth.[18] (This, of course, also echoes her immediate post-war hopes for a federal Europe.)

As events turned out, Arendt's comments on the implications of an Israeli 'victory' over her Arab neighbours in the struggle for existence, and especially on the danger of reliance on external powers (initially Britain, and then increasingly the United States), became more and more Cassandra-like:

> The growth of a Jewish culture would cease to be the concern of the whole people; social experiments would have to be discarded as impractical luxuries; political thought would center around military struggle; economic development would be determined exclusively by the needs of war.[19]

> Almost from the beginning, the misfortune of the building of a Jewish National Home has been that it was accompanied by a Central European ideology of nationalism and tribal thinking among the Jews, and by an Oxford-inspired colonial romanticism among the Arabs.[20]

> Only folly could dictate a policy which trusts a distant imperial power for protection, while alienating the goodwill of neighbors.[21]

During the 1950s, and until the writing of *Eichmann in Jerusalem*, Arendt had little to say in public about Israeli politics. She had urged a secular, economically co-operative model for development of the Jewish homeland and it had been spurned. After one of the terrorist outbreaks in the early 1950s she wrote to a friend requesting an article: 'The whole business is absolutely nauseating. I decided that I do not want to have anything to do with Jewish politics any longer.' This shift in focus should not, however, be read as a fundamental loss of commitment. She gave financial support in the war of 1967 and was proud of the Israelis' victory. Young-Bruehl sums up her ambivalence towards Israel by quoting a letter Arendt wrote after her first visit in 1935: 'I know that any real catastrophe in Israel would affect me more deeply than almost anything else.'[22]

Reflecting in 1972 on this phase of her life, Arendt underlined the personal, practical nature of her commitment, even if she did underestimate the length of her own period of active involvement:

> You know the only group I ever belonged to were the Zionists. This was only because of Hitler, of course. And this was from '33 to '43. And after that I broke. The only possibility (was) to fight back *as a Jew* and not as a human being – which I thought was a great mistake, because if you are attacked as a Jew you have to fight back as a Jew, you cannot say 'Excuse me, I am not a Jew; I am a human being.' This is silly. And I was surrounded by this kind of silliness. There was no other possibility, so I went into Jewish politics – not really politics – I went into social work and was somehow also connected with politics.[23]

Thus Arendt herself validated the analysis in *The Origins of Totalitarianism* of the political necessity of Zionism.

CHAPTER FIVE

Eichmann In Jerusalem

The outrage surrounding the publication of *Eichmann in Jerusalem* arose in part from its cumulative critique of almost all the interested parties; Arendt had simply succeeded in offending everybody. No individual or group emerges with an unblemished record. Israeli society and Israeli politicians, especially Ben-Gurion, are castigated for a series of offences from the illegality of Eichmann's kidnap to the (deliberately) poor quality of the German simultaneous translation at the trial. Other national interests, including the West Germans who washed their hands by not even making a show of requesting extradition to Germany, fare no better. The trial itself, despite the care and integrity of the judges, is criticized on a number of levels – from its weak basis in international law (Arendt, like Jaspers, preferred the idea of an international tribunal), through the failure to hear defence witnesses, to the *non sequitur* of the appeal (which revised the major conclusions of the lower court about the nature of Eichmann's participation) and the indecent haste of the execution (on the same day as the appeal for clemency was rejected).

Two apparent conclusions were, however, felt most keenly. The first arises from Arendt's analysis of the progress of the Nazis' so-called 'solutions' of the Jewish problem. Despite the fact that she seeks to limit the range of the book in both her introduction and her postscript to the second edition (we were told that it is a 'trial' report and nothing more), the bulk of it is a detailed history of the fate of European Jewry at the hands of Eichmann, his superiors and his organization. In this process a charge is repeatedly directed towards those who collaborated, who crossed 'the abyss between helping Jews to escape and helping the Nazis to deport them'.[1] 'To a Jew this role of the Jewish leaders in the destruction of their own people is undoubtedly the darkest chapter in the whole dark story.'[2] Episodes cited run the gamut from corruption (buying out named individuals), through bungling on the part of Jewish Councils (as they failed to identify the trap laid for them), to the charge of Zionist disregard of the fate of the overly assimilated. In measuring the reaction to these charges it is difficult, but I think possible, to separate the emotional from the factual. Lucy Davidowicz's seminal work, *The War Against the Jews*, examines most of Arendt's charges and the hypothesis that without Jewish complicity and assistance the numbers killed in the camps would have been dramatically cut. Her conclusion is that:

> This extraordinary argument on behalf of chaos derives from total ignorance of the historical evidence. The Germans managed with amazing facility to deport over a quarter of a million Jews from the Warsaw ghetto at this time precisely because the Jews of Warsaw were 'unorganized and leaderless'.

Davidowicz dismisses the complicity charge in the same terms as the passivity charge: 'Miss Arendt's penchant for grand philosophic schematic flourishes on her disdain for historical evidence.'[3] The emotional reaction was even more extreme:

Arendt never recovered the central position in American Jewish intellectual life which she had achieved almost at a stroke with *The Origins of Totalitarianism*.

The other major source of offence was the implication of the psychological profile of her main subject. In pointing to Eichmann's disengagement from reality, the rag-bag of metaphysical rubbish he carried in his head, his total failure to consider alternatives ('the simple fact [was] that he could see no one, no one at all, who was actually against the Final Solution'), and the totalitarian bureaucracy within which he worked ('if the thing had to be done at all', he argued, against the brutally indiscriminate killing he found in Romania, 'it was better that it be done in good order'[4]), many of Arendt's readers thought that she was not only explaining but also excusing.

Nothing, in fact, could have been farther from the truth. In the epilogue to *Eichmann in Jerusalem* Arendt draws attention to, in her view, the irony that the Israeli court, in bringing Eichmann to justice in the way that it did, failed to appreciate the true historical significance of the Holocaust: 'it appeared to prosecution and judges as not much more than the most horrible pogrom in human history.'[5] It should have become clear that 'only the choice of the victims, not the nature of the crime could be derived from the long history of Jew-hatred and anti-Semitism.'[6] Arendt's own, alternative sentence to that of the judges is in fact a philosophical attack on the concept of collective guilt ('what you meant to say was that where all, or almost all, are guilty no one is'), and a reaffirmation rather than an evasion of responsibility.

> Just as you supported and carried out a policy of not wanting to share the earth with the Jewish people and the people

of a number of other nations – as though you and your superiors had any right to determine who should and who should not inhabit the world – we find that no one, that is no member of the human race, can be expected to share the earth with you. This is the reason, and the only reason, you must hang.[7]

Excommunication

The most authoritative charge-sheet against Arendt from the Jewish establishment came in an open letter by Gershom Scholem, the historian Arendt so admired for his work on Jewish mysticism. Scholem's letter and Arendt's reply were printed in *Encounter* in January 1964. The exchange established many of the themes in the controversy already under way, and also indicates for us the extent to which the two sides were talking at cross-purposes.

Adopting the lofty, patrician tone of a teacher rebuking his student, Scholem tried to explain Arendt's lack of sympathy ('your account ceases to be objective and acquires overtones of malice') by referring to her origins:

> In the Jewish tradition there is a concept, hard to define and yet concrete enough, which we know as *Ahabath Israel*: 'Love of the Jewish people . . .' In you, dear Hannah, as in so many intellectuals who came from the German left, I can find little trace of this.

For Scholem insufficient time had passed for his generation to have the necessary perspective and objectivity to judge actions taken in the catastrophe of the Holocaust. Arendt's background and prejudice had, however, led her to presume that this was possible and to make significant errors, chiefly through her lack of sympathy. He took her to task in the case of Leo Baeck (called, in the first edition of *Eichmann*, a 'Jewish Führer' – an epithet she removed, without comment, from the second edition) and over all of the other accusations of Jewish complicity.

> There were among them [the Jewish Councils] also many people in no way different from ourselves, who were compelled to make terrible decisions in circumstances that we cannot even begin to reproduce or reconstruct. I do not know whether they were right or wrong. Nor do I presume to judge. I was not there.

Finally, Scholem disagrees about the interpretation of the trial. Finding the Court itself more convincing than Arendt's alternative judgement, he also argues that the execution was 'historically wrong', and Arendt's description of Eichmann as a 'convert to Judaism' 'a mockery'. The shift from the 'radical evil' of *The Origins of Totalitarianism* to the 'banality of evil' is unconvincing and the teacher concludes that he is unable to take the student's thesis seriously. 'I had expected, with your earlier book in mind, something different.'[8]

Arendt's reply is characteristically forthright and uncompromising. On the question of her origins she rejects the association with the left ('if I can be said to have "come from anywhere", it is from the tradition of German philosophy') and defines her personal sense of Jewish identity.

> I have always regarded my Jewishness as one of the indisputable factual data of my life, and I have never had the wish to change or disclaim facts of this kind . . . in this

> sense I do not 'love' the Jews, nor do I 'believe' in them;
> I merely belong to them as a matter of course, beyond
> dispute or argument.

Referring to the 'campaign of misrepresentation' against the book from the 'Jewish "establishment" in Israel and America', Arendt then proceeds to restate her case. In claiming that he was a 'Zionist' she had quoted Eichmann himself, indirectly, on his 'conversion'. In judging individuals' actions she had been conscious of the moral 'possibility of *doing nothing*'. Her judgements were of the individual, not groups. In a private letter to a reader she amplified this point in terms similar to the 'liberal rationalization' she had identified in *The Origins of Totalitarianism*: 'there is one important excuse for them: the co-operation was gradual and it was difficult indeed to understand when the moment had come to cross the line which never should have been crossed'.[9] The execution was '*politically* and *juridically* (and the last is all that actually mattered) correct'. However, on the question of radical evil, Scholem was right.

> It is indeed my opinion now that evil is never 'radical', that
> it is only extreme, and that it possesses neither depth nor
> any demonic dimension . . . Only the good has depth and
> can be radical.[10]

In New York, where this exchange was published, the controversy provoked civil war among the Jewish intellectual community, which for over a decade had lionized Arendt. Irving Howe, whose first job had been working for her at Schocken books, describes an open meeting called by the editors of *Dissent*.

Hundreds of people crowded into the hall where Lionel Abel and Marie Syrkin, a veteran Labor Zionist writer, spoke against Arendt's thesis, while Raul Hilberg, an authoritative scholar of the Holocaust, and Daniel Bell spoke more or less for her. We had asked Hannah herself to come, but she did not answer our letter. The meeting was hectic, with frequent interruptions: Abel furiously pounded the table; Alfred Kazin intervened nervously at the last moment to defend Arendt; Vladka Meed, a heroic survivor of the Warsaw ghetto uprising, passionately attacked Arendt's views in Yiddish; and I as chairman translated rapidly from a Yiddish speech made by a leader of the Jewish socialist Bund. Sometimes outrageous, the meeting was also urgent and afire.[11]

The sense of betrayal was palpable. Norman Podhoretz, the rising star of a conservative tendency in American Jewish commentary of which, the Eichmann controversy apart, Arendt might have emerged as the natural leader, spoke of the 'perversity of brilliance'.[12] It was felt that, even if Arendt was partly right about the actions of the Jewish leadership, more was to be lost than gained by exposing the truth. After her death these objections were subtly transmuted into an accusation of a lack of humility before what Young-Bruehl terms the 'sacred preserve' of Holocaust studies. As Walter Laqueur put it: 'Hannah Arendt was mainly attacked not for *what* she said but for *how* she said it.'[13] Most painful for her personally was the failure to achieve a reconciliation with Blumenfeld before his death in Israel in May 1963.

In fact, the empirical refutation went less smoothly than most of Arendt's detractors anticipated. The defence, and counter-accusations, were most notoriously summarized in a book by Jacob Robinson, *And the Crooked Shall Be Made Straight*, published in 1965. Robinson attempted a line-by-line refutation, not only of Arendt's analysis of Eichmann's personality and the trial, but also the statements about Jewish behaviour and the Jewish fate in specific areas and periods.[14] The problem was that far from closing the empirical argument, Robinson's alternative narrative frequently deepened and extended it. Even reviewers wishing to use the book to further their doubts about Arendt's thesis were forced to admit that in it they had forged a doubled-edged sword. At least one subsequently wrote to her to apologize, eliciting a revealing confession: 'the whole truth is that I did not know the answers myself when I wrote the book.'[15]

Arendt herself had little sympathy with the line-by-line approach. In her essay 'Truth and Politics', reprinted in the revised edition of *Between Past and Future* in 1968, she used the controversy to reflect more broadly upon the relationship of power and truth.[16] Showing how 'factual truth informs political thought' as 'rational truth informs philosophical speculation', and the brutal fact that the opposite of factual truth is the lie, she proceeds to identify the political role of the truth-teller:

> Only when a community has embarked upon organized lying on principle, and not only with respect to particulars, can truthfulness as such, unsupported by the distorting forces of power and interest, become a political factor of the first order. Where everybody lies about everything of importance, the truth-teller, whether he knows it or not has begun to act.

The essay itself turns to questions of self-deception and the cynical manipulation of mass opinion in the context of the

Cold War, but there can be no doubt of Arendt's sense of the correctness of her position in the Eichmann case:

> The political function of the story-teller – historian or novelist – is to teach acceptance of things as they are. Out of this acceptance, which can also be called truthfulness, arises the faculty of judgement.[17]

Personally, the episode tended to confirm Arendt and Blücher in a view of who their real friends were. She was in any case under emotional pressure closer to home throughout the whole incident, as a consequence of the first signs of Blücher's illness in late 1961 (he suffered an aneurism which presaged the brain haemorrhage eventually to kill him) and her own survival of a bad crash in a taxi crossing Central Park in March 1963. Howe concludes his account with another story.

> A year after the 1963 debate I ran into Hannah Arendt at a party and stretched out a hand in greeting. With a curt shake of her head and that bold grim smile of hers, she turned on her heel and walked off. It was the most skillful cut I have ever seen or received, and I was wounded quite as keenly as she wanted me to be.[18]

PART III

America:

FROM POLITICAL THEORY
TO PHILOSOPHY

CHAPTER SIX

Arendt and the American Republic

Hannah Arendt arrived in New York in 1941, a direct victim of the Nazi rise to power in Germany and the occupation of France. She was thirty-five years old. With her she brought her husband of one year, Heinrich Blücher, and they were soon joined by her mother Martha. Blücher and Martha disliked each other: he thought she was bourgeois; she thought he was untidy. Family responsibilities dominated Arendt's life at least until the death of Martha in 1948 (she died whilst on her way to visit her stepdaughter Eva in England) and Blücher's achievement in 1952 of permanent employment at Bard College. She took the lead in learning English, initially through a period spent with a host family in New England, and there seems to have been little questioning of the assumption that she would provide for them.[1]

In addition, Arendt arrived in the New World with a mission to understand and explain what had happened to the Europeans, and particularly the Germans, given added force by her direct, personal experience of totalitarianism (her arrest in Germany and her internment in France). In due course the result was *The Origins of Totalitarianism* (1951), in which Blücher's inspiration and collaboration were generously acknowledged. She also enjoyed a reputation in Zionist circles for her work in Paris on youth emigration to Palestine, which gave her her initial American work assignments: as a journalist for *Aufbau*, as an administrator for the projects associated with Jewish Cultural Reconstruction, and as an editor for Schocken books. From this platform she was able to construct the central role in American Jewry so spectacularly shattered in the reaction to *Eichmann in Jerusalem*.

These two important features of Arendt's reputation (the initial analysis of totalitarianism and her Zionist credentials) are significantly grounded in experience before her emigration and have been dealt with in Chapters Three, Four and Five. The focus of this chapter is on Arendt's interaction with American politics and society, and the effect of her adopted country on her strong self-image as a contributor to a 'German' philosophical tradition. America posed new questions for her, added new dimensions to her views about responsible political action, and prompted some unexpected reactions to contemporary controversies in the fields of race, education, and public morality. Such reactions took several forms, from the self-conscious theorizing of her works of political science, *The Human Condition* and *On Revolution*, through engaged political commentary of the type that she contributed to journals like *Dissent* and *Partisan Review*, to popular, sometimes instant journalism.

In time, Arendt derived many satisfactions from her life in America, which survived relatively unscathed from her battle royal with the Jewish establishment. In 1951, as if a reward for the success of *The Origins of Totalitarianism*, she became a citizen and soon added to this formal status an idiosyncratic delight in American slang (even some of her more formal writings are dotted with phrases like 'when the chips are down' or 'let's face the music') and other aspects of her inherited culture.[2] At least up until her death in 1975 she also enjoyed a minority following within the political-scientific community (perhaps reaching its apogee in the conference on 'The Work of Hannah Arendt' in Toronto in 1972), and a popular reputation as a commentator on contemporary America, contributing to symposia on such varied subjects as American religion, violence in American life, the death of John F. Kennedy and the Bicentennial.[3]

Over time Arendt and Blücher established a group of American friends to complement those who had shared their experience of exile and Americanization, and who survived the crisis over Eichmann. Chief among the former were the writer Mary McCarthy and the poet Randall Jarrell. McCarthy became probably Arendt's closest confidante in the last twenty years of her life after a very rocky start to their relationship as a consequence of a flippant remark she made about Hitler.[4] Arendt took Jarrell on a highly-charged exploration of German literature after he confessed to falling in love with a 'country called German', and he in turn produced a wry, affectionate portrait of the Blüchers' marriage (which he called 'the Dual Monarchy') in his campus novel *Pictures From An Institution*.[5]

As they became economically more secure Arendt and Blücher also set up a pattern for the working year. Arendt rarely taught for more than one semester in each academic session and used the remainder of the year for writing, often with grant-support, and for travelling. Some of these trips mixed business and pleasure as when she delivered the Frankfurt Peace Prize ovation for Jaspers in 1958, or received prizes herself (the Lessing Prize in 1959, the Sigmund Freud Prize in 1967, which particularly touched her because it was for excellence in German prose, and the Sonning Prize in 1974). In 1961 she took Blücher for his first post-war tour of Europe to see German friends and holiday in Italy. In the 1960s her visits with Jaspers and his wife were almost annual, and from 1967 there was a reconciliation of sorts with Heidegger.

Unlike several other distinguished intellectual refugees from Germany (for example, the members of the Frankfurt School), Arendt lived an effectively free-lance life as an academic, based in New York but supporting her work through grants and increasingly prestigious short-term contracts at the universities of Chicago, Columbia, Cornell, Princeton and Northwestern. Her early association with the New School of Social Research was cemented by an appointment to it as University Professor of Political Philosophy.[6] This was the context in which her major works of political philosophy, *The Human Condition* (1958) and *On Revolution* (1963) were produced.

The Human Condition

The Human Condition, often cited as Arendt's central contribution to political philosophy (as opposed to political science), is a dense and, at times, confusing book. Mary McCarthy, in *The New Yorker*, says that it, like *The Origins of Totalitarianism*, has 'the same faculty of surprising, then awakening suspense, and finally coming to appear as clear as daylight'.[7] Not all readers have shared her experience.

Characteristically, it begins with a disclaimer. The overall project, which Arendt calls in an evocative phrase to 'think what we are doing', is carried forward without consideration of what is meant by thinking. The book is about the *vita activa*, without conceding anything of the importance of the *vita contemplativa*.

'What we are doing' is approached through three fundamental human activities – normatively a rising hierarchy, but roughly in descending order of chronological sequence given

Arendt's black account of the modern when compared with the ancient world. The categories are: 'Labor', the biological processes which give rise to Life; 'Work', an unnatural or artificial activity in which man as *homo faber* produces things with durability and utility; and finally 'Action', which takes place between men, giving rise to 'plurality', human history and the essential conditions of political life.

Arendt's expository method of dealing with those activities relies on historical reflection ('Action reveals itself fully only to the story-teller, that is to the backward glance of the historian, who indeed always knows better what it was all about than the participant') and close etymological analysis.[8] The result is a kind of episodic western intellectual history, with some arresting angles (one effect, for example, is for her to reduce Marx to Adam Smith as both rely on the withering away of the state). Once again, there is a frontal attack on the 'pretences' of the social sciences, which in striving for prediction 'reduce man as a whole, in all his activities, to the level of the conditional and behaving animal'.[9] However, almost at the end, there is an arresting concession. As Arendt laments the victory of the *animal laborans* in the modern world, with the resulting 'striking loss of human experience', she reflects gloomily:

> The trouble with modern theories of behaviorism is not that they are wrong but that they could come true, that they actually are the best possible conceptualization of certain obvious trends in modern society. It is quite conceivable that the modern age – which began with such an unprecedented and promising outburst of human activity – may end in the deadliest, most sterile passivity history has ever known.[10]

The strong normative reference to political life in fifth-century Athens and the idealization of the *polis* make Arendt's judgements about the failure of the modern, post-revolutionary world sit uneasily with her preference for the historical method and its retrospective approach to judgement. Ultimately, the book is an appeal for the restoration of political freedom in precisely this mould, where the conditions of action can be recreated by 'love' and 'respect' (the faculty of forgiving) and by contract (the faculty of 'making and keeping promises').[11] Christianity and contract theory give a modern opportunity to recreate ancient virtues. (Another important source of redemption is art.)

The Human Condition is a semantic and scholarly *tour de force*; the range of Arendt's references and her pursuit of etymological distractions are bewildering. In so far as it eschews reflection and claims, I think inconsistently, to avoid prediction, it is, however, hard to characterize it as other than preliminary. As she explains in the 'Prologue':

> 'What we are doing' is indeed the central theme of this book. It deals only with the most elementary articulation of the human condition, with those activities that traditionally, as well as according to current opinion, are within the range of every human being. For this and other reasons, the highest and perhaps purest activity of which men are capable, the activity of thinking, is left out of those present considerations.[12]

On Revolution

On Revolution (1963) was a direct contribution to an important 1960s genre in political science: the comparative study of revolution. To this debate Arendt brought a vigorous critique of one of the most popular assumptions: the idea, articulated by Robert Palmer, that there was an ideologically uniform 'Atlantic Revolution' linking the late eighteenth-century experiences of America and France.

Echoing categories from *The Human Condition*, Arendt offers both a definition of revolution and a critical history of the phenomenon since the eighteenth century. Revolution, like war, implies violence and hence for Arendt is out of the political realm. The outcome of the violent act is, however, potentially constructive. As a beginning (or 'natality') it can create conditions for genuine freedom.

From a historical perspective, what the book becomes is a party political broadcast on behalf of the American Revolution; Bernard Crick has called it 'an act of gratitude'.[13] To summarize: revolution as the 'Constitutio Libertatis' (the goal of the United States) worked; as the 'Novus Ordo Saeculorum' (in France, and in an even more perverted form in the Bolshevik Revolution) it was doomed to failure. America's was a unique achievement, attained under peculiar conditions, including an absence of general poverty and a high degree of political sensitivity (which for Arendt meant knowledge of the classics). In the course of the French Revolution the term was, in contrast, irrevocably debased as the revolutionary leaders failed a number of moral and political tests, chiefly through their seduction by the ideas of historical 'necessity' and their switching of the agenda from the political to social questions. This is Arendt's most direct comment on the Palmer thesis:

> It is odd indeed to see that twentieth-century American even more than European learned opinion is often inclined to interpret the American Revolution, or to criticize it because

> it so obviously did not conform to lessons learned from the latter. The sad truth of the matter is that the French Revolution, which ended in disaster, has made world history, while the American Revolution, so triumphantly successful, has remained an event of little more than local importance.[14]

In the Russian case, and especially through what is for Arendt the illogical concept of 'permanent revolution', the outcomes are even more catastrophic. In imitating the 'course of events' of the French Revolution rather than the 'men' of the American Revolution, the Bolsheviks became victims of ideology and the architects of terror. What they learned was 'history and not action' (the latter directly in terms of *The Human Condition*): 'they were fooled by history, and they have become the fools of history.'[15]

What this means, of course, is that the normative standard against which both achievements and debasements are tested is a profoundly conservative concept of the political. Genuine revolutions are in fact more restorations than new dawns. Political freedom is only guaranteed in circumstances of direct personal participation, achieved in the *polis*, and possibly recoverable by a modern, historically sensitive élite.

> Finally, it is perfectly true, and a sad fact indeed, that most so-called revolutions, far from achieving the 'Constitutio Libertatis', have not even been able to produce constitutional guarantees of civil rights and liberties, the blessings of 'limited government', and there is no question that in our dealings with other nations and governments we shall have to keep in mind that the distance between tyranny and constitutional, limited government is as great as, perhaps greater than the

distance between limited government and freedom. But these considerations, however great their practical relevance, should be no reason for us to mistake civil rights for political freedom, or to equate these preliminaries of civilized governments with the very substance of a free republic. For political freedom, generally speaking, means the right 'to be a participator in government, or it means nothing'.[16]

It is no accident that Arendt's revolutionary heroes are Jefferson, with his ideal of small 'elementary republics', the semi-anonymous leaders of French revolutionary councils and twentieth-century workers' communes, and the leaders of the Hungarian uprising of 1956.

Between Past and Future

By the early 1960s, then, Arendt had marked out for herself a distinctive place in the field of political philosophy, structured around a personal interpretation of the intellectual history of the West and some trenchant views on the condition of genuine (or responsible) political action. The collection which best encapsulates her achievement at this stage, which she herself once confessed she considered her best book, is entitled *Between Past and Future: Eight Exercises in Political Thought* (1961). Early on in its life she had thought of developing it into a textbook to be called *Introduction to Politics*.[17] Although at first glance many of the issues which engage her in these essays are the stuff of immediate political controversy (her own reactions to the *Eichmann* controversy, for example, or the Space Race and 'progressive education'), she also took this opportunity to anthologize some weightier work (on concepts of 'tradition', 'history', 'authority', and 'freedom') and to introduce them with an important synthetic study of 'the gap between past and future'.[18] Methodologically, the essays promise exercises and experience in 'how to think'. Here Arendt borrows a 'parable' from Kafka, about a traveller caught on a road of time.

> He has two antagonists: the first presses him from behind, from the origin. The second blocks the road ahead. He gives battle to both. To be sure, the first supports him in his fight with the second, for he wants to push him forward, and in the same way the second supports him in his fight with the first, since he drives him back.

From this dilemma emerges the notion of an ideal vantage point, yet one that is based in the experience of the struggle.

> His dream, though, is that some time in an unguarded moment – and this would require a night darker than any night has ever been yet – he will jump out of the fighting line and be promoted, on account of his experience in fighting, to the position of umpire over his antagonists in their fight with each other.[19]

The ideal observation point of the umpire, together with its connotation of judgement, seems close to Arendt's personal target of experientially informed but independent understanding. It matches her identification elsewhere of the 'spectator' and the story-teller as guardians of important insights. It also looks forward to some of her concerns in *The Life of the Mind* including the difficulty of achieving such a platform from which to judge: 'we seem neither equipped nor prepared for this activity of thinking, of settling down in the gap between past and future.'[20]

Substantively, this goal is embedded in a set of essays which give a characteristic intellectual history. Arendt begins with the ancient virtues, and notes their adaptation by the Christian tradition (with a stirring account of the efficacy of the doctrine of hell) and the impact of modern science (especially through concepts of process rather than form and progress rather than cycles). The metaphysical mistakes of the eighteenth and nineteenth centuries (including Hegel's 'gigantic effort' at synthesis) then collapse into the arbitrariness, meaninglessness and confusion of the modern world.[21] In sum, what has happened is the simultaneous 'recession of both freedom and authority in the modern world', and of the conditions which explain a 'chain of catastrophes touched off by World War I', most significantly, of course, the example of totalitarianism.[22]

Constructively, Arendt is concerned to show the fleeting moments of genuine political action revealed by this survey, first in 'polis-life, which to an incredibly large extent consisted of citizens talking with one another' and then in times of 'foundation' or 'beginning' like the Roman Republic and the American Revolution.

> For if I am right in suspecting that the crisis of the present world is primarily political, and that the famous 'decline of the West' consists primarily in the decline of the Roman trinity of religion, tradition and authority, with the concomitant undermining of the specifically Roman foundation of the political realm, then the revolutions of the modern age appear like gigantic attempts to repair those foundations, to renew the broken thread of tradition, and to restore, through founding new political bodies, what for so many centuries had endowed the affairs of men with some measure of dignity and greatness.[23]

Political Controversy

Arendt's reactions to American affairs on the ground make most sense in terms of this idealization of the generation of the founding fathers as responsible for a new beginning. Their texts, supplemented by de Tocqueville's *Democracy in America*, read through the lens of her own ideas about political responsibility and political action, explain effectively her stance on questions of foreign policy, race, education, cultural renewal, student protest and political ethics. Sometimes these reactions were in the liberal mainstream, sometimes they seemed perversely authoritarian, but they did have the merit of self-consistency. Most of them were composed against a backdrop of appreciation for her adopted country which had largely escaped 'the monstrosities of the century' that inspired so much of her political theory. America seemed relatively immune to 'dark times'. 'Dark Times . . . were perhaps unknown in American history, which otherwise has its fair share, past and present, of crime and disaster.'[24]

For many traditional commentators Arendt was an enigma when it came to foreign affairs and especially the condition of Europe. The elision of Stalinism and Nazism in *The Origins of Totalitarianism*, together with what was perceived as a principled cultural conservatism, apparently made her a natural candidate for co-option into the rhetoric of the Cold War.[25] In her own writings, however, she strove, generally successfully, to maintain her respect for cultural traditions and to welcome political progressivism.

In the immediate post-war years, as debate swirled around the question of European reconstruction, she held out some hopes for leadership by the former resistance movements in a federal Europe, and for Europe itself as a 'middle way'. Only through this means could the damage done by the collapse of the pre-war class structure ('in its feudal form in the East' and 'its bourgeois form in the West') be overcome.[26]

Such hopes were rapidly overcome by events, and Arendt spent much of the early 1950s explaining to Americans Europe's misgivings over the polarization of the Great Powers and the threat of the atomic bomb. In a series of articles in *Commonweal* she demonstrated the roots of anti-Americanism in envy (the 'radical difference in exterior circumstances') and as a focus for pan-European nationalism. Neither side was portrayed as entirely rational: the Americans with their reliance on 'destructive technicalization' and the Europeans with their tendency (so disastrous in the inter-war years) to retreat into the private sphere, as well as their failure to recognize that hostility to Americanization was in fact dread of the 'emergence of the modern world'. Together these presented the 'world's central problem today': 'the political organization of mass societies and the political integration of technical power'.[27]

Even as divisions in Europe hardened Arendt was reluctant simply to take sides. She had seen loyalty become conformity and had witnessed processes like the McCarthyite investigations before. As apostasy, confession and recrimination became commonplace, she urged a powerful distinction between professional 'ex-communists' (like Whittaker Chambers, the accuser of Alger Hiss) and 'former communists' who 'neither looked for a substitute for a lost faith nor (concentrated) all of their efforts and talents on the fight against Communism'. This was a distinctly European perspective: Arendt knew at first hand what the party had meant to many of her associates in their efforts to retain political and personal dignity. The role of the 'convert' from communism, particularly as an 'expert' on the phenomenon itself, deeply troubled her as he sought 'to apply this training to a new cause after the old cause has disappointed him'. A genuinely free society had to protect itself against the 'makers of history', whether they were informed by the ideological cause of communism or that of 'democracy'.[28]

In thinking about the Cold War Arendt saw the struggle on a different kind of historical scale: 'the present conflict between the two parts of the world may well be decided by the simple question of which side understands better what is involved and what is at stake in revolution.'[29] In one way this formulation was a return to the superiority of the American Revolution argued for in *On Revolution*, but it was also a comment on the conduct of the Cold War. Not only are there immense risks in the kind of 'hypothetical warfare' implied in the arms race but the rhetoric of the Cold War disguises what are at root personal and economic issues.

> Short of war and short of total annihilation, both of which I fear will remain actual dangers, the position of the West and of the United States in particular will depend to a considerable extent upon a clear understanding of these two factors involved in revolution: freedom and the conquest of poverty.

In other words 'revolution involves both liberation from necessity so that men may walk in dignity and constitution of a body politic that may permit them to act in freedom.'[30]

Running through all of these comments on international affairs is a consistent thread, connecting Arendt's day-to-day views with her political science. The scourge is that of nationalism, and the great virtue of the United States that it 'has never been a nation-state and therefore has been little affected by the vices of nationalism and chauvinism'.[31]

America does, however, suffer another 'national' vice: that of racism. Conventional liberals also had trouble with Arendt's views of race and ethnicity. Here there was a conflict between two world views *par excellence*: that of the American liberal, whose conscience is regularly tested by the disparity between constitutional guarantees and the failure to meet legitimate black claims on them; and that of the cosmopolitan European intellectual, well-versed in the subtleties of class, national and regional origin, and accustomed to systematic and enduring inequality.

Arendt's writings are studded with negative comment on black protest, black power and the black revolution; frequently she comes close to blaming the victims of discrimination for the strength of the backlash they are likely to invoke.[32] There was, however, a firm philosophical spine to her objections to the aims and means of much of the protest. Controversy over her position reached its head in 1959 when a piece she had written on the enforced desegregation of Arkansas schools, 'Reflections on Little Rock', was rejected by *Commentary*, which had commissioned it, and published eventually in *Dissent*.

The outrage centred ostensibly on Arendt's refusal to accept educational desegregation as a legitimate target for the civil rights campaign. She had attracted criticism, for example, for the assertion that 'marriage laws (anti-miscegenation statutes) in 29 of the 49 states constitute a much more flagrant breach of letter and spirit of the Constitution than segregation of schools.' In an emotional preface, Arendt declared that to accuse her of lack of sympathy was to miss the point.

> Like most people of European origin I have difficulty in understanding, let alone sharing, the common prejudices

of Americans in this area. Since what I wrote may shock good people and be misused by bad ones, I should make it clear that as a Jew I take my sympathy for the cause of the Negroes as for all oppressed or underprivileged peoples for granted and should appreciate it if the reader did likewise.³³

But Arendt sticks to her guns. Her main point was not that American society was blameless – indeed she pointed to the irony of race relations as a moral blot in a society which had failed to participate in the racism of imperialism and colonialism ('the one great crime in which America was never involved') – but that clear distinctions needed to be made between the political, social and private spheres. Education belongs firmly to the social sphere where discrimination is natural: 'what equality is to the body politic . . . discrimination is to society.' Focusing on a news picture of a rejected black child walking the gauntlet of taunts and abuse from white children, she found the drama poignantly unjust. 'Have we now come to the point where it is the children who are being asked to change or improve the world? And do we intend to have our political battles fought out in the school yards?'³⁴

The key question for Arendt is 'not how to abolish discrimination, but how to keep it confined within the social sphere, where it is legitimate, and prevent its trespassing on the political and the personal sphere, where it is destructive'. 'Purely social' spheres of free association (such as hotels, as well as schools) should be exempt from legislation, unlike public services (such as transport), as should the 'private' relationship of marriage. Arendt faced segregated hotels with equanimity: 'just as I see no reason why other resorts should not cater to a clientele that wishes not to see Jews while on holiday'. 'Not discrimination, and social segregation, in whatever forms, but racial legislation constitutes the perpetuation of the original crime in this country's history.'[35] Similarly offensive to American liberals was Arendt's instinctive respect for the rights of individual states, as local expressions of political feelings.[36]

The most charitable interpretation of these views is that they are insufficiently sensitive to the goals of the victims of discrimination, in the service of a categorical distinction stretched beyond its links. They are, however, consistent with Arendt's more direct comments on American public education as a service, in which she lambasted 'the widespread, uncritical acceptance of a Rousseauian ideal'.[37]

Her educational views were unashamedly conservative. Among her targets were ideas about the 'existence of a child's world', 'the science of teaching', and the substitution of 'doing for learning'. 'The function of the school is to teach children what the world is like and not to instruct them in the art of living.' The sphere-of-interest point is safeguarded by separating the process of education from politics, 'because in politics we always have to deal with those who are already educated'.[38] It is hard to imagine a set of ideas with which Arendt could be more out of step with her normal political allies.

Such divergences were not often articulated at this stage. With her connections in Europe and America, as well as her growing role as a political commentator, Arendt was naturally drawn into the ferment of political revolt of 1968. In the official reaction to opposition to the Vietnam War, as revealed in the 'Pentagon Papers', she had little hesitation in finding another totalitarian spectre. In her famous essay 'Lying in Politics', which she delivered as a speech at several universities and summarized for the op-ed page of the *New York Times*, the continuum between 'lying in principle' and the demands of public relations and 'problem-solving' is mercilessly exposed:

> This deadly contribution of the 'arrogance of power' – the pursuit of a mere image of omnipotence, as distinguished from our aim of world conquest, to be attained by non-existent unlimited resources – with the arrogance of mind, an utterly irrational confidence in the calculability of reality, became the leitmotif of the decision-making processes from the beginning of escalation in 1964.[39]

The strength of the language represents a strong fear, set out more abstractly in her contemporaneous essay, 'On Violence'. As 'authority' recedes the possibility of violence advances: 'every decrease in power is an open invitation to violence – if only because those who hold power and feel it slipping from their hands, be they the government or be they the governed, have always found it difficult to resist the temptation to substitute violence for it.'[40]

In these circumstances Arendt's admiration for the architects of civil disobedience and passive protest are unequivocally expressed. An 'extraordinarily strong, highly qualified and well-organized' domestic opposition could revive the best in the American political tradition, in particular by realizing a Tocquevillian vision of political authority. 'Consent, in the American understanding of the term, relies on the horizontal version of the social contract and not on majority decisions.' Arendt's American version of the Workers' Councils, which she had so admired in the European context, was the same network of voluntary associations which other liberal historians and social scientists of the 1950s and 1960s such as Richard Hofstadter were simultaneously rediscovering. At its most extreme this enthusiasm led her to suggest a special constitutional provision for voluntary associations and special interest groups, and to inquire 'whether it would not be possible to find a recognized niche for civil disobedience in our institutions of government'.[41]

In more immediate, practical terms Arendt thus expressed solidarity with the student revolt of the late 1960s – up to a point: 'psychologically this generation seems everywhere characterized by sheer courage, an astounding will to action, and by a no less astounding confidence in the possibility of change.' In April 1968 she addressed the student sit-in at Columbia, an experience which moved her deeply. However, the students had manifestly failed to build alliances outside the university and should, Arendt said, beware of undermining the foundation of the institutions which enabled their protest.[42] If the university itself were to be destroyed it would 'spell the end of the whole movement'.[43]

In time the practice of American politics came to realize Arendt's worst fears. Her bicentennial essay for the *New York Review of Books* (1975), based on an address given in Boston, had a title strongly redolent of the experience of Vietnam and Watergate: 'Home to Roost'. After such an 'outright humiliating defeat', as well as other foreign policy disasters and 'manifold domestic troubles', there was a danger that Americans might follow inter-war Germany into a flight to the 'reassurance of day-to-day life'. 'Image-making' and 'lying on principle' had come to America, and even after the resignation of Richard Nixon, Gerald Ford had not much more to offer than an appeal to amnesia. As Arendt concluded: 'I rather believe with Faulkner: "the past is never dead, it is not even past".'[44]

In summary, then, Arendt's views of American politics, culture and society were profoundly ambivalent. On the one hand there is her jeremiad against the impact of mass society, through, for example, advertising and the manipulation of public taste, and its corrosion of the conduct of politics.[45] On the other hand she remained optimistic about the robustness and vitality of a participative democracy. As she put it in a lecture in 1948, she had a feeling of wonder that 'a Twentieth Century (and in some senses a Nineteenth Century) society lives and thrives on the solid basis of an Eighteenth Century political philosophy'.[46] What this survey of her daily political and social commentary points to most directly is the difficulty she presents to any attempt to characterize her work. In interviews and public lectures she gave late in life Arendt relished the discomfort of interrogators who tried to pigeon-hole her and her work. But she never deserted her admiration for the founding fathers, and what could be made of their heritage.

CHAPTER SEVEN

The Life of the Mind

The early 1970s were personally and emotionally difficult for Arendt, but intellectually liberating. In February 1969 she lost Jaspers, and in October 1970 Blücher, who died suddenly, just two years after his retirement from Bard. She had tried to steel herself for both events, but they none the less disturbed her equilibrium significantly. Matters were not helped by a proposal of marriage from a dishevelled W. H. Auden, whom she had known and admired since the late 1950s. In 1973 Auden himself died, and she found herself in a cycle of memorial services. From this resulted a pact with Anne Weil that when the first of the two died the other should not feel compelled to travel to the funeral. In the event she did not have to keep her side of the bargain.[1]

In her work, however, Arendt was poised to take on new challenges. Initially, these were conceptualized as a development of *The Human Condition*, which had concentrated on the *vita activa*, towards the *vita contemplativa*. As she announced in Toronto in 1972, 'this *Human Condition* needs a second volume and I'm trying to write it.'[2]

A more practical stimulus was the invitation earlier that year to deliver the Gifford Lectures at the University of Aberdeen. As she was aware, this had been a platform from which a distinguished series of American philosophers (notably Josiah

Royce, William James and John Dewey) had addressed their British and European counterparts. Her first series on 'Thinking' was delivered in 1973. Early in the second series on 'Willing', begun in 1974, she suffered a heart attack. On 4 December 1975 she died suddenly in her New York apartment after dinner with friends. In her typewriter was a page with the title and two epigrams for 'Judging'. In 1978 'Thinking' and 'Willing', together with the transcript of some lectures on Kant (which she assumed to contain the substance of 'Judging') were published by Mary McCarthy as her literary executor.

Philosophical credentials

Arendt always disliked being described as a 'philosopher'. Replying to a television interviewer in 1964 she declared: 'I am not a philosopher. My profession – if it can be called that – is political theory. I have bid philosophy my final farewell. As you know, I did study philosophy, but that does not mean that I have stuck to it.'[3] What seemed to disturb her most was the appropriation by 'professional' philosophy of the business of thinking, and of thinking about thinking, which in her scheme of things was a human necessity. She explained this further in the 1972 Toronto symposium:

> Reason itself, the thinking ability which we have, has a need to actualize itself. The philosophers and the metaphysicians have monopolized this capability. This has led to very great things. It also has led to rather unpleasant things – we have forgotten that every human being has a need to think, not to think abstractly, not to answer the ultimate questions of God, immortality and freedom, nothing but to think while he is living.[4]

Before we can decide what Arendt was if she was not a philosopher we need to consider other things that she manifestly was not. Despite her regular attendance at and contributions to the American Political Science Association, she was not really a recognized political scientist; her distrust of behavioural science and her approach to empirical evidence precluded that.[5] She might have had some claim as a literary critic, although her approach (as in *The Origins of Totalitarianism*) was a fairly utilitarian one; she went to literature to confirm philosophical and historical truth. She might have liked to be a poet or story-teller, the *Dichter* whom she most admired, but left no imaginative work beyond her unpublished poems. To be a historian was probably the next best thing, but again the selectivity of her approach and the powerful subordination of evidence to interpretation ruled against this. She remained something of a theologian, building on the legacy of her graduate study. Her most emphatic counter-claim was that of the political theorist, but, as I hope to show below, her approach in this field was fundamentally philosophical.

Her work reflects a rich and highly personal mixture of all of these elements. She herself once described her method as pearl-fishing (*Perlenfischerei*), although she was probably thinking of Walter Benjamin when she did so.[6] But chiefly, in my view, the work strives towards and finally, in this last phase, becomes philosophy.

It does so through a complex layering process. In the beginning, and remaining as a substrate throughout, there is the 'German' tradition of language, literature and ideas described in Chapter Two. Throughout her life she identified with the 'existential' pole of the Kantian legacy noted there, and in particular with the achievement of Heidegger (one of her key concerns about *Thinking*, Volume I of *The Life of the*

Mind, was the personal effect its implied criticism of her now very elderly mentor might have). Later, she worked backwards through the alternative stream, through Marx to Hegel, and attempted a kind of reconciliation. Her final work, described in this chapter, anticipates that of one of her most significant critics and admirers, Jürgen Habermas, in its concern for political action in a moral context and the goal of intersubjectivity.[7]

The second significant layer in Arendt's work is thus the battle with Marx, and other theorists of the Left, which began in the 1930s particularly in Paris, and continued into the 1950s with her writing of *The Human Condition*. By the early 1970s she was ready for a final confrontation with Hegel, once an adversary kept at arm's length but later an ally.

As she became more and more committed to history as an explanatory device the greatest philosopher of history had become more and more of a concrete obstacle, no longer to be dismissed polemically (as she did when she called him the 'last ancient philosopher' in 'What is Existenz Philosophy?').[8] Her task may have been made significantly easier by the fact that Blücher, who would have been most sceptical of the exercise, was dead. But in any case, by the time of the Toronto discussions Arendt was prepared to set out her philosophical stall in no uncertain terms. This is how she concludes her statement on reason and thinking:

> So in this respect it may even be nice that we lost the monopoly of what Kant once very ironically called the professional thinkers. We can start worrying about what thinking means for the activity of acting. Now I will admit one thing. I will admit that I am, of course, primarily interested in understanding. This is absolutely true. And I

will admit that there are other people who are primarily interested in doing something. I am not. I can very well live without doing anything. But I cannot live without trying at least to understand whatever happens.

And this is somehow the same sense in which you know it from Hegel, namely where I think the central role is reconciliation – reconciliation of man as a thinking and reasonable being. This is what actually happens in the world.[9]

The Life of the Mind

We can deduce Arendt's purpose in writing *The Life of the Mind* from its structure. Although the completed sections include a relentless denunciation of 'professional philosophy' and its practitioners, the aim is apparently a traditional one: to set out accounts of the most important mental activities or faculties, and to indicate their relationship in an integrated philosophy of mind.[10] As is inevitable in an ambitious project no more than half finished and composed under the constraints of illness and anxiety, the work can be criticized (perhaps more than any other of Arendt's) for its self-referential qualities, its ignorance of other technical developments, as well as its final lack of coherence. I hope to show, however, that the purposes of the whole are more coherent than the sum of the surviving parts and bear a closer relationship to Arendt's previous work than many (including those still impressed by the earlier work in political theory) are prepared to allow.

In execution *The Life of the Mind* is anything but a display of metaphysical abstraction. The first volume, *Thinking*, is, for example, an essay on *thoughtlessness* and its consequences. In introducing it Arendt refers specifically to her discovery, through Eichmann, of the 'banality of evil' and the resulting hypothesis that thought may help to condition us against evil and evil-doing.

> If . . . the ability to tell right from wrong should turn out to have anything to do with the ability to think, then we should be able to 'demand' its exercise from every sane person, no matter how erudite or ignorant, intelligent or stupid, he may happen to be.[11]

This question sparks another reference back to a former work, *The Human Condition*, and its aim to 'think what we are doing'. Arendt's project here is to discover 'what we are "doing" when we think'.[12]

The initial thrust of Arendt's investigation is epistemological and, characteristically, concerned with distinctions. Accepting the impossibility of arriving at a 'region beyond appearances' or the plurality of the images and facts which bombard us, she is concerned to establish how, without 'leaving' or 'transcending' the world, we can withdraw from it to think and arrive at meaning. Questions about meaning are more profound than the common-sense conclusions of science or the products of reason and intellect. For example, they ask not what something is but 'what it means for it to be'.[13]

Thus her main concern is with a process and the conditions under which it (and the other two faculties in her triptych) can operate. A prime condition is the withdrawal alluded to above. All of the faculties require 'dispassionate quiet' in order to function. In the case of thinking there are also more precise prerequisites: a willingness to 'prepare the particulars' by de-sensing them, or standing back from a specific engagement with them; the cultivation of imagination, as in the ability to develop metaphor and story-telling; and, above all, a sympathetic quality which Arendt calls love.[14]

All of this is independent of the technical, and for her misguided, search for truth of the 'philosophers'. A theme which runs through the exposition is the incapacity of traditional epistemology from Plato through Kant to involve the self fully in the act of thinking: 'it is this helplessness of the thinking ego to give an account of itself that has made the philosophers, the professional thinkers, such a difficult tribe to deal with.'[15] Genuine thinking is an internal dialogue, in which the plurality of society is replaced by the duality of the individual, a 'two-in-one dialogue between me and myself'. 'Thinking, existentially speaking, is a solitary but not a lonely business: solitude is that human situation in which I keep myself company.'[16] Temporally, it also involves a return to the 'gap' which Arendt identified (after Kafka) in *Between Past and Future*, where time is suspended for thinking to operate.[17] It is a universal and necessary human characteristic: universal because (against Socrates) it cannot be confined just to the few, and necessary because we cannot live responsibly without it. 'Unthinking men are like sleepwalkers.'[18]

Just as *Thinking* is in fact about the consequences of not thinking and the conditions of humanity, *Willing*, the second, less polished volume, is about the condition and obligations of freedom. 'A will that is not free is a contradiction in terms.'[19] In methodological terms Arendt switches from epistemology to her own brand of the history of ideas. There are three broad phases in her account of the history of the will. First the Greek world was able, by and large, to exist without the concept except in some embryonic forms, such as Aristotle's idea of *pro airesis* (where it exists as the choice between alternatives). Secondly, the will itself was discovered by

Augustine (the first Christian, and, for Arendt, the only Roman philosopher) as a necessary foundation for spiritual individuality. This inaugurated a theologically based tradition which survived through to Kant. Finally, the nineteenth century, supposedly the higher point of the doctrine of the Will, in fact saw its demise as Nietzsche repudiated the assumption of free choice and Heidegger opened the question of willing 'not to will'.[20]

For Arendt the Augustinian insight is central and survives subsequent attacks.

> It was the experience of an imperative demanding *voluntary* submission that led to the discovery of the Will, and inherent in this experience was the wondrous fact of a freedom that none of the ancient peoples – Greek, Roman or Hebrew – had been aware of, namely that there is a faculty in man by virtue of which, regardless of necessity and compulsion, he can say 'Yes' or 'No', agree or disagree with what is factually given, including his own self and his existence, and that this faculty may determine what he is going to do.[21]

From this basis the will functions freely not just as a choice between alternatives (the ancient legacy of the *liberum arbitrium* – 'the free choice between willing and nilling'), but also as a capacity for *beginning*, with profound political implications.[22] In the postscript to *Thinking* Arendt described willing as dealing with the subject matter of 'projects' not objects. The focus of the will is on particulars, action, and spontaneity. Again, the professional philosophers have missed the point: 'political freedom is distinct from philosopher's freedom in being clearly a quality of the I–can and not the I–will.' As such it only really happens in communities and achieves its highest expression in the act of foundation.[23]

It is clear from the design of the overall work that *Thinking* and *Willing* were intended to be preliminary to the faculty of judgement, which would both include and transcend the lower-level faculties. The hierarchy is referred to several times in the first two volumes, notably when in *Thinking* Arendt refers to judging as bringing the general and the specific together.[24] It is reasonable to assume that in *Judging* she intended to give us a final word on the search for standards, for the 'inner compass' of the imagination to which she had referred in one of her first American essays.[25] Looking forward, again in *Thinking*, she separates consciousness (or the realm of thinking) from conscience (the proper goal of judgement):

> Its criteria for action will not be the usual rules, recognized by multitudes and agreed upon by society, but whether I shall be able to live with myself in peace when the time has come to think about my deeds and words. Conscience is the anticipation of the fellow who awaits you if and when you come home.[26]

In so far as this goal represents the most important and consistent thrust of Arendt's entire work, the fact that *Judging* remains incomplete is a tragedy. All we have to give a lead as to its contents is two epigrams typed on the title-page and the mass of her contemporaneous notes. Several scholars, notably Michael Denneny (writing before the publication of *The Life of the Mind*), McCarthy herself, Ronald Beiner, and Young-Bruehl, have attempted this task, with efforts that converge on an agreed agenda, but which, in my view, are finally unsatisfactory.[27]

Like McCarthy, who reprinted what she could find as an

appendix to *The Life of the Mind*, both Denneny and Beiner see the answer as lying in Arendt's work on Kant. She was simultaneously giving lectures on Kant's political philosophy (at Chicago and elsewhere) and leading a seminar at the New School. In fact, in an irony noted by Beiner, reconstructing Arendt on judgement is a task remarkably similar to that faced by Arendt herself in reconstructing Kant. In both cases we have strong *prima facie* evidence that a series of aesthetic insights were intended to assume political importance. In the first case, the trail was ended by Kant's senility; in the latter case, by Arendt's death.[28]

In an extended essay accompanying his edition of Arendt's teaching notes on Kant, Beiner advances the thesis that Arendt's concept of judgement shifted in the early 1970s, at the same time as her concentration on the *vita activa* transferred to the *vita contemplativa*. In his view this explains a number of changes of emphasis in her writing: from political agency in the plural society to elevation of 'spectatorship' and the 'abyss of individual freedom'. Tracing her writings on the subject from 'Understanding and Politics' (1953) to the 'unwritten treatise' of the third volume of *The Life of the Mind*, he sees the replacement of an active concern with the persuasive impact of judgement (as in the unequivocal statement in *Between Past and Future* that 'judging is one, if not the most important activity in which this sharing-the-word-with-others comes to pass') to a more passive concern with judgement as disclosing truth.[29]

By the time of the essay 'Thinking and Moral Considerations' (1971) the merger between political and aesthetic realms, between action and art, is almost complete. Arendt develops an analogy between thinking and consciousness, and judging and conscience:

> If thinking, the two-in-one of the soundless dialogue, actualizes the difference within our identity as given in consciousness and thereby results in conscience as its by-product, then judging, the by-product of the liberating effect of thinking, realizes thinking, makes it manifest in the world of appearances, where I am never alone and always much too busy to be able to think. The manifestation of the wind of thought is no knowledge; it is the ability to tell right from wrong, beautiful from ugly. And this indeed may prevent catastrophes, at least for myself, in the rare moments when the chips are down.[30]

Kant's elaboration of a type of 'reflective judgement' where individual cases would have 'exemplary validity', via imagination, taste and the concept of a *sensus communis*, was decisive for Arendt's thought. It enabled her to develop an assumption about the intersubjective validity of judgements (although one which several critics, including Habermas, pointed out had no secure cognitive status).[31]

In positing his two-stage model Beiner allies these insights with an acceptance by Arendt of a more passive role of the individual against the broad sweep of history. 'The life of the mind reaches its ultimate fulfillment not in the comprehensive vision of metaphysics, as it did for the ancients, but in the disinterested pleasure of the judging historian, poet, or story-teller.'[32]

Is the shift exaggerated? In all we have of the *ur-text* (the epigrams), as opposed to the editorial reconstructions, I think the evidence is ambiguous. The first epigram is from Cato: 'the victorious cause pleases the Gods but the defeated one pleases Cato.' Arendt often used it in her lectures to emphasize the superior role of the judging spectator against the rigid systematization of progressive historical schemes like Hegel's. The second is a stanza from Goethe's *Faust*, translated by Beiner as follows:

> If I could remove the magic from my path,
> And utterly forget all enchanted spells,
> Nature, I would stand before you but a man,
> Then it would be worth the effort of being a man.

The concepts in the last two lines – 'ein Mann allein' and 'ein Mensch zu sein' – together with Arendt's other favourite Kantian reference to 'Selbsdenken' or thinking for myself (also a key concept for Lessing), underline the critical importance of reaching judgements as part pf the process of becoming truly human. The emphases of both of Beiner's stages are about 'being-at-home in the world', and the juxtaposition of political action versus contemplation as acceptable outcomes may be overdrawn.[33]

There seems little doubt that Arendt's final goal was a moral and hence (for her) political role for judging, in which all of her previously articulated values such as love, imagination and communicability could play their part. As Denneny quotes from the lectures, Kant's mistake was in 'withholding questions of right and wrong from the sphere of reflective (aesthetic) judgement'.[34] My conclusion is that she was aiming for a concept much wider and more capable of stimulating action than 'pleasure in the beautiful'.[35] At a conference on her work in January 1973 she said 'the reason why I believe so much in Kant's *Critique of Judgement* is not because I am interested in aesthetics but because I believe that the way in which we say "that is right, that is wrong" is not very different from the way in which we say "this is beautiful, this is ugly".'[36] Arendt never finally achieved the synthesis, also to elude Kant, nor is there clear evidence that she could have done given more time.

Reviews and obituaries

The circumstances in which *The Life of the Mind* was produced, together with its incomplete condition, meant that reactions to Arendt's death were frequently intertwined with an attempt to come to terms with this final statement. Most obituaries turn out to be extended, often puzzled, reviews of her work.

Broadly there were three types of responses: concern that the project was not complete, coupled with speculation about how it might have developed; identification of her partial achievement; and, in some voices (perhaps fewer than would have been the case fifteen years earlier), recognition of an original and significant contribution.

Sheldon Wolin, reviewing *The Life of the Mind* in the *New York Review of Books*, is an archetype of the first position. For him the work 'is characteristically Arendtian, which is to say that there are passages of remarkable insight and suggestiveness, just as there are others that seem wrong-headed and unsupported by fact, text or reason'.

The balance is, however, positive, as Wolin takes Arendt's sense of contribution to a philosophical lineage seriously ('Kant-Fichte-Hegel-Nietzsche-Heidegger'-Arendt) and struggles to define a kind of 'politics of the mind' that will recognize her concern for public affairs in this complex elaboration of the more solitary processes of the inner life. For him the book works as a protest against Heideggerian 'passivity', even if it is steeped in the melancholy of a recognition that this protest may not be effective.

> But those who have read her writings will remember Hannah Arendt not only as a writer of remarkable insight and intelligence, but one of rare courage who took on the gravest and most dangerous problems of the times. A momentary flash of this memorable past is provided by a phrase she used in these volumes, 'man the fighter'. Perhaps this, rather than those 'Hellenizing ghosts' that Nietzsche warned against should be the epitaph to the life of her mind.[37]

Wolin took Arendt seriously as a philosopher and as a historian of ideas. The 'yes but' school tended to come more from political science and to expose some of the difficulties of aligning her political philosophy with empirical studies. Martin Jay's splendid contribution to the *Partisan Review* collection 'Hannah Arendt: Opposing views' is a good example.

Jay admires Arendt for her instinct for important issues, her elevation of political theory over political science (and her influence on contemporary thinkers such as Habermas), as well as her positive view of freedom. But he is also deeply critical of her élitism and her view of Marx (as the 'straw man' of the Second International). Not only does she misread Marx, by accusing him of reducing all politics to socio-economic issues, but she neglects other important themes in twentieth-century Marxist scholarship. In other words, her attempted revival of political existentialism fails: 'what must finally be recognized is that the version of the human condition on which all her work rested will simply not wash.'[38]

The committed Arendtians leapt to her defence. Most accused her critics of simply not understanding the premises. Leon Botstein responds to Jay in the *Partisan Review* by accusing him of failing 'to grasp Arendt's own method and intent as an intellectual of *praxis*, for whom speech and action had an effective place within the events which surrounded her writing'.[39] An important plank for the defence was the claim for Arendt's 'method', and its phenomenological connection of the individual and the world of facts. A high point of the genre is another obituary-review by Ernst Vollrath, which concludes with a typical Arendtian epigram: 'Understanding always relates to the phenomenal communality of the world.'[40] Perhaps the final word should rest with her life-long friend, Hans Jonas, who at her memorial service said: 'to call her a great thinker is for none of her contemporaries to presume, nor to predict how her thought will withstand the onslaught of time.'[41]

Postscript

What, philosophically, had Arendt achieved before her death? Most of the questions posed, but not fully answered, by her four 'ground-clearing' works have to do with what is called in *Eichmann in Jerusalem* the concept of an 'unmastered past'.[1] In other words, the work urges a recognition that we ought, as human beings, to have answers to the questions she poses: 'How could it happen? Why did it happen?'

Methodologically, I propose three main ways in which the philosophical interpretation scores over the political. It relies upon the accuracy of at least the following perceptions of her work. First, that she was throughout her life temperamentally more inclined towards Hegel than towards Marx (she certainly recognized in preparing her Gifford Lectures that she would have to come to terms with Hegel). In Hegel not only does understanding come with philosophy, but also understanding of a type which dialectically combines the subjective and the objective – a task which comes close to characterizing the thrust of almost all of Arendt's work. Second, it makes more of Arendt's perspective as a phenomenologist (or, as she chose to put it, a philosopher of *Existenz*) than those who pursue the political angle are able to do. Young-Bruehl describes her as once saying to a student: 'I am a sort of phenomenologist, but not in Hegel's way – or Husserl's.'[2] Third, it implies a more purposive unity for the corpus: that, faced with the political and moral catastrophes of the twentieth century, Arendt sought to secure a platform from which to understand what has happened to us (the project of 'thinking what we are doing'), the detachment which this implies, and the qualifications to assign responsibility and to judge.

Substantively, I am tempted at the moment to conclude that the project was a heroic failure. She did, however, give some effective philosophical pointers about what would constitute adequate answers to these dilemmas. She urged that the answers should be specific (the phenomenology is relevant here), that in moral terms they should be normative and not merely contextual, and that they should make sense in the evolution of western thought and society. She never fully synthesized these conflicting requirements, and it is not clear that she would have succeeded in doing so in a completed *The Life of the Mind*.

Nevertheless, my interpretation shifts the focus to this incomplete, posthumously published work. It relies upon identification of the earlier work as essential but preliminary: *The Origins of Totalitarianism* as establishing the historical and sociological background of the major crisis of our century; *The Human Condition* as critically separating the *vita activa* (on which it concentrates) from the *vita contemplativa* (to which Arendt finally aspired); *The Origins of Revolution* as showing the necessity for escape from 'social' pressures of the type which overwhelmed the French and Russian Revolutions (even if this escape goes no further than the constitutional, or 'political' emphases of the American Revolution); and, crucially from this point of view, *Eichmann in Jerusalem*, which in a pivotal sense explores the conditions of judgement of human action in the most extreme case. *The Life of the Mind* is itself divided into three volumes – *Thinking*, *Willing*, and *Judging*. My conclusion is that this dialectical formulation – thinking, willing, judging – can stand as a structure for Arendt's work and what she made of the experiences of her life.

This interpretation is not a unification of the corpus around a programmatic intention of which the author was self-consciously aware. Rather, I see it as a sympathetic account of the shifting focus of the work which preserves, incrementally, selected achievements of each of the separate books. It leaves us with Arendt in metaphysics and epistemology, areas which, until she steeled herself to deliver the Gifford Lectures, she had tried to avoid. It also then perhaps explains a series of powerful affective, rather than intellectual, reactions to Arendt's work, and why to such large groups of her readers, independent of Jewish political orthodoxy and Oxford-based academic snobbery, her books were persuasive and important. At the very least it causes some of the other objections to her theory and the terms in which it is cast to fall.

Why is any of this important? Chiefly, I believe, because historians and philosophers have major difficulties in thinking about the existential crises of the twentieth century. Looking back they have evidence of the unthinkable and of the inexplicable in the Holocaust. Looking forward they have the prospect of the unthinkable in the threat of nuclear annihilation, however much the Cold War has thawed as we move through the 1990s. In dealing with these dilemmas Arendt gave us no secure answers (nor is there any assurance that she would have done so if she had finished the project that I believe she started). I contend, however, that her efforts deserve more serious consideration than we are generally prepared to allow them today.

This conclusion prompts some final thoughts on Arendt's short-lived but stellar career. Her concerns, and her personal approach, were briefly and spectacularly in the mainstream but are unquestionably no longer so. How did she create this reputation, and how did she lose it? Or, to allow for more contextualist possibilities, and to modify a metaphor from Alfred Kazin, what circumstances allowed her to occupy centre stage, and then switched off the lights?

I suggest that there is more in these questions than intellectual fashion. It is, in fact, hard to suppress the personal contributions. Much of the force of Arendt's writings, sometimes on the most abstruse topics, comes from a sense of felt experience. In the context of the European war, its origins and its aftermath, hers was a voice from the front line. Occupying this position Arendt was also able to be discovered by, and progressively to cultivate, some important constituencies: the Jewish diaspora; emigré German intellectuals, and American political liberals. As Arendt's friend Alfred Kazin described the self-image of their generation of Jewish immigrants in the 1950s: 'But it was the best of times for Jewish intellectuals who, as Robert Lowell said with as much truth as spite, "were unloading their European baggage". Yes, we Jews were *older*; we embodied "a school of experience". We had been stage center at all the great intellectual dramas and political traumas of this century.'[3]

In this process the mystique that characterized much of the exposition of Arendt's ideas was more of an asset than a liability. Her writings, with their idiosyncratic mixture of empathy (for the stateless and 'homeless in the modern world', for example) and austerity (as in anything that required an etymological distinction) had just the right impact: they felt right and sounded complex. Finally, when all these elements were working positively for her, her independence and apparent uniqueness (as an academic maverick) added to her reputation and her influence. Irving Howe describes the effect she had on him and others of his generation:

> She made an especially strong impression on intellectuals – those who, as mere Americans, were dazzled by the immensities of German philosophy. But I always suspected that she impressed people less through her thought than the style of her thinking. She bristled with intellectual charm, as if to reduce everyone in sight to an alert discipleship . . . Whatever room she was in Hannah filled through the largeness of her will; indeed she always seemed larger than her setting. Rarely have I met a writer with so acute an awareness of the power to overwhelm.[4]

The reactions reflect almost directly the obverse of all of these attributes. First there was the loss of the constituencies: principally the Jewish reaction to *Eichmann in Jerusalem*, but also that of the German philosophers as she and Jaspers (to say nothing of Husserl and Heidegger) went out of style. It was not long before German intellectuals (presaging the *Historikerstreit*) preferred political accommodation to painful acknowledgement of an unsatisfactory past. Even the vaguely left-wing American school of journalism which had taken her to its heart found some of her reflections on race and political activism hard to take. Simultaneously, there was a recession of the issues which had been so important to her. With the development of the Cold War the idea, for example, of 'western' refugees was suddenly less attractive.

What this added up to was a loss of popular momentum. As the tide turned, being an imperfectly understood loner became less of an attraction, more an excuse for disregard. Socially it meant that in the last years of her life and the immediate aftermath of her death the circle of Arendt's friends (the inner council or, as Young-Bruehl has identified them, the 'tribe') became less of a launching-pad and more of a laager. It is hard to say that much has changed. As the comments on recent writings about Arendt in the Bibliography below suggest, enthusiasm for her work is now patchy and partial, and does little to confirm her true importance in the history of western ideas.

References

Preface

1. Derwent May, *Hannah Arendt* (Harmondsworth: Penguin, 1986), p. 70.
2. Anthony Quinton, 'Hannah Arendt' in Alan Bullock and R. B. Woodings (eds.), *The Fontana Biographical Companion to Modern Thought* (London: Fontana, 1983), p. 19.
3. Stuart Hampshire, 'Metaphysical Mists', *Observer* (30 July 1978), p. 26.
4. Margaret Canovan, *The Political Thought of Hannah Arendt* (London: Methuen, 1977), pp. 43, 121.
5. Melvyn A. Hill (ed.), *Hannah Arendt: The Recovery of the Public World* (New York: St Martin's Press, 1979), p. x.
6. See, for example, Hannah Arendt, 'Letter' in *New York Review of Books* (1 January 1970), p. 36.
7. Elisabeth Young-Bruehl, *Hannah Arendt: For Love of the World* (New Haven and London: Yale University Press, 1982), p. 98.
8. Hill, *op. cit.*, p. 322.
9. Richard Bernstein, 'Hannah Arendt: The Ambiguities of Theory and Practice', in Terence Ball (ed.), *Political Theory and Praxis: New Perspectives* (Minneapolis: University of Minnesota Press, 1977), pp. 141–58; see also his *Philosophical Profiles: Essays in a Pragmatic Mode* (Cambridge: Polity Press, 1986), pp. 221–59.
10. Young-Bruehl, *op. cit.*, pp. 109–10.

Chapter One

1. Young-Bruehl, *Hannah Arendt*, pp. 50–6.

2. Hannah Arendt, *Rahel Varnhagen: The Life of a Jewish Woman* (New York and London: Harcourt Brace Jovanovich, 1974) (Hereafter *RV*), pp. xiii, xv.
3. Young-Bruehl, *op. cit.*, p. 57.
4. *Ibid*, p. 100.
5. *RV*, p. 215.
6. *RV*, pp. 13, 153-4, 181, 225.
7. *RV*, pp. 25, 112-13, 188.
8. *RV*, pp. 50, 163, 168.
9. *RV*, pp. xvii, 84-5, 219; Hannah Arendt, *The Origins of Totalitarianism* (London: André Deutsch, 1986) (Hereafter *OT*), pp. 59, 221.
10. *RV*, pp. 58, 221.

Chapter Two

1. Young-Bruehl, *Hannah Arendt*, pp. 490-500.
2. *Ibid*, p. 493.
3. Alfred Kazin, *New York Jew* (London: Secker and Warburg, 1978), p. 199.
4. '*Eichmann in Jerusalem*: an exchange of letters between Gershom Scholem and Hannah Arendt', *Encounter* (January 1964), pp. 51-6.
5. Hannah Arendt, 'What is Existenz Philosophy?', *Partisan Review*, 8:1 (1946), pp. 34-56.
6. *Ibid*, pp. 38-40.
7. *Ibid*, p. 41.
8. *Ibid*, pp. 43, 45.
9. *Ibid*, pp. 46-50.
10. *Ibid*, pp. 53-5.

Chapter Three

1. Hannah Arendt, *Men in Dark Times* (London: Jonathan Cape, 1970) (Hereafter *MDT*), p. 45.
2. *OT*, pp. vii, xxiv.
3. Young-Bruehl, *Hannah Arendt*, p. 203.
4. *OT*, p. 392.
5. *OT*, p. 120.

6. Examples are J. A. Hobson on imperialism and Isaac Deutscher on Stalin.
7. *OT*, pp. 187, 208, 218–20.
8. *OT*, pp. 475, 478.
9. Young-Bruehl, *op. cit.*, p. 211.
10. Canovan, *op. cit.*, p. 47; see also the judgement of Richard H. Pells in *The Liberal Mind in the Conservative Age: American Intellectuals in the 1940s and 1950s* (Middletown: Wesleyan University Press, 1989) p. 96: 'Couched in the dispassionate language of the social sciences, it was in reality a powerful jeremiad–and a moving autobiography by someone who continued to believe in the old-fashioned principles totalitarianism had nearly destroyed.'
11. *OT*, pp. 363-4.
12. *OT*, p. 183.
13. *OT*, p. 440.
14. Young-Bruehl, *op. cit.*, p. 324; *OT*, p. 443.
15. *OT*, p. 459.
16. Hannah Arendt, 'Organized Guilt and Universal Responsibility', reprinted in Roger W. Smith, *Guilt: Man and Society* (Garden City: Anchor Books, 1971), p. 257.
17. *Ibid*, p. 259.
18. *Ibid*, p. 262.
19. *Ibid*, p. 266.
20. *Ibid*, p. 263.
21. *Ibid*, p. 261.
22. *Ibid*, p. 265.
23. *Ibid*, p. 267.
24. *Ibid*.
25. Hannah Arendt, 'Personal Responsibility under Dictatorship', *Listener* (6 August 1964), p. 185.
26. *Ibid*, p. 186.
27. *Ibid*, p. 187.
28. *Ibid*, p. 205.
29. Karl Jaspers, *The Question of German Guilt* (Westport: Greenwood Press, 1978), p. 25; see also Young-Bruehl, *op. cit.*, p. 216.
30. Jaspers, *op. cit.*, pp. 31–2.
31. *Ibid*, pp. 39–42.
32. *Ibid*, pp. 63–74, 82–90.

33. *Ibid*, pp. 73-4, 118.
34. Karl Jaspers and Rudolf Augstein, 'The Criminal State and German Responsibility: A Dialogue', *Commentary*, 41 (1966), p. 35.
35. *Ibid*, p. 37.
36. Hannah Arendt 'Martin Heidegger at 80', *New York Review of Books* (21 October 1971), pp. 50-4.
37. *MDT*, p. ix.
38. *MDT*, p. 72.
39. *MDT*, p. 86.
40. *MDT*, pp. 11, 17, 19, 136.
41. *MDT*, p. vii.
42. *MDT*, p. 62.
43. *MDT*, p. 171.
44. *MDT*, pp. 150, 261.
45. *MDT*, pp. 209, 227, 236; see also the *New York Times* (28 March 1970), p. 25.
46. *MDT*, p. 211.
47. *MDT*, pp. 4-7.
48. *MDT*, pp. 104-5.
49. *MDT*, p. 65.
50. *MDT*, p. 50.
51. Hannah Arendt, 'The Aftermath of Nazi Rule: Report from Germany', *Commentary*, 10 (1950), pp. 342, 358.
52. Ralf Dahrendorf, *Society and Democracy in Germany* (New York: Anchor Books, 1969), p. 339.
53. Young-Bruehl, *op. cit.*, p. 130.
54. Hannah Arendt, 'The Image of Hell', *Commentary*, 2 (1946), p. 294.
55. *Ibid*, p. 292; see also Hannah Arendt, 'Introduction' to Bernd Naumann, *Auschwitz* (London: Pall Mall Press, 1966), pp. xi-xxx.
56. Quoted in Gordon A. Craig, 'The War of the German Historians', *New York Review of Books* (15 January 1987), pp. 16-19; see also Craig's 'Facing up to the Nazis', *New York Review of Books* (2 January 1989), pp. 10-15; Geoff Eley, 'Nazism, Politics and the Image of the Past', *Past and Present*, 121 (1989), pp. 170-208; and Anson Rabinach, 'The Jewish Question in the German Question', *New German Critique*, 44 (1988), pp. 159-87.
57. Quoted in Craig, 'The War of the German Historians', p. 18.

Chapter Four

1. *OT*, p. 3.
2. *OT*, p. 54.
3. *OT*, pp. 66-8.
4. *OT*, pp. 87, 92, 120.
5. Hannah Arendt, *The Jew as Pariah*, ed. Ron H. Feldman (New York: Grove Press, 1978) (Hereafter JP), pp. 29-31; 'Zionism Reconsidered', reprinted in Michael Selzer ed., *Zionism Reconsidered* (London: Collier Macmillan, 1970), pp. 224-6.
6. 'Zionism Reconsidered', pp. 226-30.
7. Hannah Arendt, ed., Bernard Lazare, *Job's Dungheap* (New York: Schocken Books, 1948), pp. 5-11.
8. Young-Bruehl, *Hannah Arendt*, pp. 188-9.
9. *Ibid*, pp. 138-48.
10. *Ibid*, p. 127.
11. *Ibid*, pp. 173-9.
12. *Ibid*, p. 186.
13. *Ibid*, p. 188.
14. *Ibid*, p. 178-9, 225.
15. *JP*, pp. 178-222, 188.
16. For a contemporary comment on this position see Mizi Paz, 'The Outsider', *Davar* (8 September 1989), p. 24.
17. Young-Bruehl, *op. cit.*, pp. 230-4.
18. *Ibid*, p. 180.
19. *JP*, p. 187.
20. *JP*, p. 203.
21. 'Zionism Reconsidered', p. 248.
22. Young-Bruehl, *op. cit.*, pp. 139, 291.
23. Hill, *Hannah Arendt*, p. 334.

Chapter Five

1. Hannah Arendt, *Eichmann in Jerusalem* (Harmondsworth: Penguin, 1976) (Hereafter EJ), p. 11.
2. *EJ*, p. 117.
3. Lucy Davidowicz, *The War Against the Jews* (New York: Holt, Rinehart and Winston, 1975), pp. 125, 429.

4. *EJ*, pp. 116, 190.
5. *EJ*, p. 267.
6. *EJ*, p. 269.
7. *EJ*, p. 279.
8. '*Eichmann in Jerusalem*: an exchange of letters between Gershom Scholem and Hannah Arendt', *loc. cit.*, pp. 51-3.
9. Young-Bruehl, *Hannah Arendt*, p. 345.
10. '*Eichmann in Jerusalem*: an exchange', pp. 53-6.
11. Irving Howe, *A Margin of Hope* (London: Secker and Warburg, 1983), p. 274.
12. Norman Podhoretz, 'Hannah Arendt on Eichmann: A Study in the Perversity of Brilliance', *Commentary*, 36 (1963), pp. 201-8.
13. Young-Bruehl, *op. cit.*, p. 472.
14. Jacob Robinson, *And The Crooked Shall Be Made Straight* (New York: Macmillan, 1965), *passim*.
15. *JP*, pp. 260-74; Young-Bruehl, *op. cit.*, p. 367.
16. Hannah Arendt, *Between Past and Future* (Harmondsworth: Penguin, 1977) (Hereafter *BPF*), pp. 227-64.
17. *BPF*, pp. 251, 256, 262. It is noteworthy that Arendt was quick to leap to the defence of others she suspected of the same kind of fate. An example is her championing of the young playwright Rolf Hochhuth whose *The Deputy* accused the papacy of politically-motivated silence about the fate of German Jews and aroused strong Catholic antagonism. See her '*The Deputy*: Guilt by Silence', *New York Herald Tribune* magazine (23 March 1964), pp. 6-9.
18. Howe, *op. cit.*, p. 295.

Chapter Six

1. Young-Bruehl, *Hannah Arendt*, pp. 164-6.
2. One comment on the collected edition of Dwight MacDonald's *Politics*, which she reviewed in the *New York Review of Books* (1 August 1968), pp. 31-3, was that 'MacDonald's batting average for short-time predictions was not too good.'
3. The Toronto symposium is summarised in Hill, *Hannah Arendt*, pp. 301-39; for other references see: 'Religion and the Intellectuals: a Symposium', *Partisan Review*, 17 (1950), pp. 113-16; 'Kennedy and After', *New York Review of Books* (26 December 1963), p. 10;

'Lawlessness is inherent in the Uprooted', *New York Times* magazine (24 April 1968), p 24; 'Home to Roost', *New York Review of Books* (26 June 1975), pp. 3-6.

4. See Carol Gelderman, *Mary McCarthy: A Life* (London: Sidgwick and Jackson, 1989), pp. 153-6.
5. *MDT*, 263-7; Randall Jarrell, *Pictures From An Institution* (London: Faber & Faber, 1954), pp. 140-96.
6. This chair, now called the Hannah Arendt Professorship of Philosophy, is currently occupied by Agnes Heller.
7. Mary McCarthy, *The New Yorker* (1959).
8. Hannah Arendt, *The Human Condition* (Chicago: University of Chicago Press, 1958) (Hereafter *HC*), p. 192.
9. *HC*, p. 45.
10. *HC*, p. 322.
11. *HC*, p. 237.
12. *HC*, p. 12.
13. Young-Bruehl, *op. cit.*, p. 403.
14. Hannah Arendt, *On Revolution* (Harmondsworth: Penguin, 1973) (Hereafter *OR*), pp. 55-6.
15. *OR*, p. 58.
16. *OR*, p. 218.
17. Young-Bruehl, *op. cit.*, pp. 325, 473.
18. *BPF*, pp. 3-15.
19. *BPF*, pp. 7, 14.
20. *BPF*, p. 13.
21. *BPF*, pp. 38, 64, 78.
22. *BPF*, pp. 26, 87, 92, 100.
23. *BPF*, pp. 51, 123, 136, 140.
24. *MDT*, p. xi.
25. On Arendt as a 'conservative' see Pells, *The Liberal Mind*, pp. 83-5, and Kazin, *New York Jew*, p. 196.
26. Hannah Arendt, 'Approaches to the "German Problem" ', *Partisan Review*, 12:1 (1945), pp. 93, 106.
27. Hannah Arendt, 'Europe and America: Dream and Nightmare', *Commonweal*, 60:23 (1954), p. 554; 'Europe and the Atom Bomb', *Ibid*, 60:24, p. 578; 'The Threat of Conformism', *Ibid*, 60:25, p. 610.
28. Hannah Arendt, 'The Ex-Communists', *Commonweal*, 57:24 (1953), pp. 595-9.

29. Hannah Arendt, 'The Cold War and the West', *Partisan Review*, 29:1 (1962), p. 11.
30. *Ibid*, pp. 18, 20.
31. Hannah Arendt, *On Violence* (London: Allen Lane, 1970) (Hereafter *OV*), p. 85; 'Lawlessness is inherent in the Uprooted', *loc. cit.*
32. *OV*, pp. 18, 63, 76.
33. Hannah Arendt, 'Reflections on Little Rock', *Dissent*, 6:1 (1959), pp. 45-6.
34. *Ibid*, pp. 50, 51. She later conceded that she had under-estimated the formative nature of the child's experience, in an exchange with Ralph Ellison. See Young-Bruehl, *op. cit.*, p. 316.
35. *Ibid*, pp. 51, 52, 181.
36. Young-Bruehl, p. 311.
37. 'Reflections on Little Rock', p. 46.
38. *BPF*, pp. 173-96.
39. Hannah Arendt, *Crises of the Republic* (New York: Harcourt Brace Jovanovich, 1969) (Hereafter *CR*), p. 39; 'Washington's "Problem-Solvers" – Where They Went Wrong', *New York Times* (5 April 1972), p. 45.
40. *OV*, p. 87.
41. *CR*, pp. 46, 92, 99.
42. *OV*, pp. 15, 24.
43. *CR*, p. 208.
44. 'Home to Roost', *loc. cit.*
45. *BPF*, pp. 197-226.
46. Young-Bruehl, p. 210.

Chapter Seven

1. Young-Bruehl, *Hannah Arendt*, p. 465.
2. Hill, *Hannah Arendt*, p. 306.
3. Young-Bruehl, *op. cit.*, p. 327.
4. Hill, *op. cit.*, p. 303.
5. Young-Bruehl, *op. cit.*, p. 390.
6. *Ibid*, p. 95.
7. Jürgen Habermas, 'Hannah Arendt's Communications Concept of Power', *Social Research*, 44 (1977), pp. 3-24.

8. 'The Philosophy of Existenz', *loc. cit.*, p. 39.
9. Hill, *op. cit.*, p. 303.
10. Hannah Arendt, *The Life of the Mind* (London: Secker and Warburg, 1978), 2 vols. *Thinking* and *Willing* (Hereafter *LM* I and *LM* II), I, pp. 69-70, 80, 92, 166; II, p. 4.
11. *LM* I, pp. 4, 13.
12. *LM* I, p. 8.
13. *LM* I, p. 57.
14. *LM* I, pp. 70, 76, 103, 177.
15. *LM* I, pp. 166-7.
16. *LM* I, p. 185.
17. *LM* I, pp. 202-6.
18. *LM* I, pp. 181, 191.
19. *LM* II, p. 14.
20. *LM* II, pp. 15, 60, 84, 158, 172.
21. *LM* II, p. 21.
22. *LM* II, p. 109.
23. *LM* I, p. 213; II, pp. 200, 204.
24. *LM* I, p. 69.
25. Hannah Arendt, 'Understanding and Politics', *Partisan Review*, 20:4 (1953), p. 391.
26. *LM* I, p. 192.
27. Michael Denneny, 'The Privilege of Ourselves: Hannah Arendt on Judgment', in Hill, *op. cit.*, pp. 245-76; Mary McCarthy in *LM* II, pp. 255-72; Ronald Beiner ed., *Hannah Arendt: Lectures on Kant's Political Philosophy* (Chicago: University of Chicago Press, 1982), pp. 89-156; Young-Bruehl, *Mind and the Body Politic* (New York and London: Routledge, 1989), pp. 24-47.
28. Beiner, *op. cit.*, p. 91.
29. *Ibid*, pp. 89-156.
30. Hannah Arendt, 'Thinking and Moral Considerations: A Lecture', *Social Research*, 38:3 (1971), pp. 445-6.
31. Beiner, *op. cit.*, p. 137.
32. *Ibid*, p. 144.
33. Denneny, *op. cit.*, p. 247; Beiner, *op. cit.*, p. 126.
34. Denneny, *op. cit.*, p. 260.
35. *LM* II, p. 268.
36. Young-Bruehl, *Hannah Arendt*, p. 452.

37. Sheldon Wolin, 'Stopping to Think', *New York Review of Books*, (26 October 1978), pp. 18–21.
38. Martin Jay, 'Hannah Arendt: Opposing Views', *Partisan Review*, 45 (1978), pp. 356, 368.
39. *Ibid*, p. 369.
40. Ernst Vollrath, 'Hannah Arendt and the Method of Political Thinking', *Social Research*, 44:1 (1977), p. 180.
41. Quoted in Young-Bruehl, *Hannah Arendt*, p. xxi.

Postscript

1. *EJ*, p. 283.
2. Young-Bruehl, *Hannah Arendt*, p. 405.
3. Kazin, *New York Jew*, p. 191.
4. Howe, *A Margin of Hope*, p. 270.

Bibliography

I have listed in Section A below the editions of works by Arendt referred to in the notes to my text, together with the relevant abbreviations. All of the major works with the exception of *The Life of the Mind* are currently available in paperback. Section B lists articles and other materials by Arendt of which I have made direct use in the text, also in chronological order. This is, of course, just a selection from Arendt's complete bibliography, in English and German, listed on pages 535-47 of Elisabeth Young-Bruehl's *Hannah Arendt: For Love of the World*. Although it contains the odd minor error, Young-Bruehl's bibliography is an invaluable resource, particularly useful in its indication of where and how material was subsequently recycled by Arendt herself. I have not listed separately work which appears in collected or anthologized form.

Consideration of the secondary material (Section C) must also begin with Young-Bruehl's magisterial 'philosophical biography', in comparison to which Derwent May's *Hannah Arendt* is a brief and anecdotal summary. Other interpretations listed fall into the camps listed towards the end of Chapter Seven: the enthusiasts (for example Whitfield and Hill), the constructively critical (like Bernstein, Kateb and Parekh) and the dismissive for varying reasons (like Quinton, Hampshire and Podhoretz).

More recent critical work on Arendt has shyed away from the overarching interpretations familiar in the late 1970s and early 1980s. Recent journal and anthologized material, of which a sample is included here, has tended to flow down three channels: the attempt retrospectively to co-opt Arendt into a new-style feminist philosophy, stressing affective rather than strictly rational values and methods; the continued potency of the 'official' Jewish countercharge to her views of Eichmann, the Jewish councils and the state of Israel; and finally, a series of technical commentaries, particularly on her work on Aristotle and Kant. The first theme Arendt would have had no time for. Since reviewing Alice Rühle-Gerstel's *The Contemporary Women's Problem* in Berlin in the early 1930s she was always uncomfortable with the notion of a special feminist sphere or series of attributes (see Young-Bruehl, *Hannah Arendt*, pp. 96ff., 238 and 272). On the second theme she felt she had said her final words in her reply to Scholem and in 'Truth and Politics', although there is evidence that, privately, the controversy continued to cause her pain. The final, technical currency of her work would have given her satisfaction and pride.

In Section C I have listed all of the works referred to directly or indirectly in the text, alphabetically by author or source. As with Arendt's own work I have not given separate entries for anthologized or collected articles, so I recommend that particular attention is given to items like the volume of *Social Research* dedicated to writings about her.

A. Books by Arendt

Der Liebesbegriffe bei Augustin (Berlin: J. Springer, 1929).

Lazare, Bernard, *Job's Dungheap: Essays on Jewish Nationalism and Social Revolution*, introduction by Hannah Arendt (New York: Schocken Books, 1948). *JD*

The Origins of Totalitarianism, (London: André Deutsch, 1986). *OT*

Rahel Varnhagen: The Life of a Jewish Woman, trans. by R. and C. Winston, (New York and London: Harcourt Brace Jovanovich, 1974). *RV*

The Human Condition (Chicago: University of Chicago Press, 1958). *HC*

Between Past and Future: Eight Exercises in Political Thought (Harmondsworth: Penguin, 1977). *BPF*

Jaspers, Karl, *The Great Philosophers*, volume I *The Foundation*, volume II *The Original Thinkers*, ed. Hannah Arendt (London: Rupert Hart-Davies, 1966).

On Revolution (Harmondsworth: Pelican, 1973). *OR*

Eichmann in Jerusalem: a Report on the Banality of Evil (Harmondsworth: Penguin, 1976). *EJ*

Jaspers, Karl, *The Future of Germany*, foreword by Hannah Arendt (Chicago and London: University of Chicago Press, 1967).

Benjamin, Walter, *Illuminations*, introduction by Hannah Arendt (New York: Harcourt Brace, 1968).
Crises of the Republic (New York: Harcourt Brace Jovanovich, 1969). *CR*
On Violence (London: Allen Lane, 1970). *OV*
Men in Dark Times (London: Jonathan Cape, 1970). *MDT*
The Jew as Pariah: Jewish Identity and Politics in the Modern Age, ed. Ron H. Feldman (New York: Grove Press, 1978). *JP*
The Life of the Mind, 2 vols. ed. Mary McCarthy (London: Secker and Warburg, 1978). *LM*

B. Articles by Arendt

'Franz Kafka: A Revaluation', *Partisan Review*, 11:4 (1944), pp. 412–22.
'Approaches to the "German Problem"', *Partisan Review*, 12:1 (1945), pp. 93–106.
'Zionism Reconsidered', in Michael Selzer (ed.), *Zionism Reconsidered: the Rejection of Jewish Normalcy* (London: Collier Macmillan, 1970), pp. 213–49.
'The Image of Hell', *Commentary*, 2:3 (September 1946), pp. 291–5.
'The Ivory Tower of Common Sense', *The Nation*, (October 1946), pp. 447–9.
'What is Existenz Philosophy?', *Partisan Review*, 8:1 (1946), pp. 34–56.
'Religion and the Intellectuals: A Symposium', *Partisan Review*, 17 (February 1950), pp. 113–16.
'The Aftermath of Nazi Rule: Report from Germany', *Commentary*, 10 (October 1950), pp. 342–53.
'The Ex-Communists', *Commonweal*, 57:24 (1953), pp. 595–99.
'A Reply' (to Eric Voegelin's review of *OT*), *The Review of Politics*, 15 (1953), pp. 76–84.
'Understanding and Politics', *Partisan Review*, 20:4 (1953), pp. 377–92.
'Europe and America: Dream and Nightmare', *Commonweal*, 60:23 (1954), pp. 551–4.
'Europe and the Atom Bomb', *Commonweal*, 60:24 (1954), pp. 578–86.
'The Threat of Conformism', *Commonweal*, 60:25 (1954), pp. 607–10.
'Reflections on Little Rock', *Dissent*, 6:1 (1959), pp. 45–56.
'A Reply to Critics', *Dissent*, 6:2 (1959), pp. 179–81.
'The Cold War and the West', *Partisan Review*, 29:1 (1962), pp. 10–20.

Contribution to 'Kennedy and After', *New York Review of Books* (26 December 1963), p. 10.

'*Eichmann in Jerusalem*: an exchange of letters between Gershom Scholem and Hannah Arendt', *Encounter* (January 1964), pp. 51–56.

'*The Deputy*: Guilt by Silence', *New York Herald Tribune* magazine (23 March 1964), pp. 6-9.

'Personal Responsibility under Dictatorship', *Listener* (6 August 1964), pp. 185-7, 205.

'Introduction' to Bernd Naumann, *Auschwitz: A Report on the Proceedings against Robert Karl Ludwig Mulka and others before the Court at Frankfurt* (London: Pall Mall Press 1966), xi–xxx.

'Lawlessness is inherent in the Uprooted', contribution to 'Is America by Nature a Violent Society?', *New York Times* magazine (24 April 1968), p. 24.

'He's All Dwight', *New York Review of Books* (1 August 1968), pp. 31–3.

'Letter' commenting on review of *BPF* and *MDF* by J. M. Cameron (6 November 1969), *New York Review of Books* (1 January 1970), p. 36.

'Martin Heidegger at 80', *New York Review of Books* (21 October 1971), pp. 50-4.

'Thinking and Moral Considerations: A Lecture', *Social Research*, 38:3 (1971), pp. 417–46.

'Washington's "Problem-Solvers" – Where they went wrong', *New York Times* (5 April 1972), p. 45.

'Reflections: Remembering Wystan H. Auden', *New Yorker* (20 January 1975), pp. 39-46.

'Home to Roost: A Bicentennial Address', *New York Review of Books* (26 June, 1975), pp. 3-6.

'Public Rights and Private Interests: In Response to Charles Frankel', in M. Mooney and F. Stuber, (eds.), *Small Comforts for Hard Times: Humanists on Public Policy* (New York: Columbia University Press 1977), pp. 103-8.

'Hannah Arendt: From an Interview' (with Roger Errera), *New York Review of Books* (26 October 1978), p. 18.

C. *Secondary material*

Ball, Terence (ed.), *Political Theory and Praxis: New Perspectives* (Minneapolis: University of Minnesota Press, 1977).

Beiner, Ronald, *Hannah Arendt: Lectures on Kant's Political Philosophy* (Chicago: University of Chicago Press, 1982).

Bernauer, James W. (ed.), *Amor Mundi: Explorations in the Faith and Thought of Hannah Arendt* (Boston, Dordrecht and Lancaster: Martinus Nijhoff, 1987).

Bernstein, Richard J., *Philosophical Profiles* (Cambridge: Polity Press, 1986).

Bowen-Moore, Patricia, *Hannah Arendt's Philosophy of Natality* (London: Macmillan, 1989).

Bradshaw, Leah, *Acting and Thinking: the Political Thought of Hannah Arendt* (Toronto: University of Toronto Press, 1989).

Les Cahiers du Grif, 33:3 (Spring 1986), special edition 'Hannah Arendt'.

Les Cahiers de Philosophie, 4 (Autumn 1978), special edition 'Hannah Arendt: Confrontations'.

Canovan, Margaret, *The Political Thought of Hannah Arendt* (London: Methuen, 1974, 1977).

Clarke, Barry, 'Beyond the "Banality of Evil"', *British Journal of Political Science*, 10:4 (1980), pp. 417–39.

Dahrendorf, Ralf, *Society and Democracy in Germany* (New York: Anchor Books, 1969).

Davidowicz, Lucy S., *The War Against the Jews* (New York: Holt, Rinehart and Winston, 1975).

Eley, Geoff, 'Nazism, Politics, and the Image of the Past: Thoughts on the West German *Historikerstreit*, 1986-87', *Past and Present*, 121 (1989), pp. 170–208.

Gelderman, Carol, *Mary McCarthy: A Life* (London: Sidgwick and Jackson, 1989).

Hampshire, Stuart, 'Metaphysical Mists', *Observer* (30 July 1978), p. 26.

Hill, Melvyn A. (ed.), *Hannah Arendt: the Recovery of the Public World* (New York: St Martin's Press, 1979).

Hinchman, Lewis P. and Hinchman, Sandra K., 'In Heidegger's Shadow: Hannah Arendt's Phenomenological Humanism', *Review of Politics*, 46 (1984), pp. 183–211.

Howe, Irving, *A Margin of Hope: An Intellectual Autobiography* (London: Secker and Warburg, 1983).

Jarrell, Randall, *Pictures from an Institution: A Comedy* (London: Faber & Faber, 1954).

Jaspers, Karl, *The Question of German Guilt*, trans. by E. B. Ashton (Westport, Conn.: Greenwood Press, 1978).

Jaspers, Karl and Augstein, Rudolf, 'The Criminal State and German Responsibility: A Dialogue', *Commentary*, 41 (1966), pp. 33-9.

Jay, Martin, 'Hannah Arendt: Opposing Views', *Partisan Review*, 45 (1978), pp. 348-68.

Kaplan, Gisela T. and Kessler, Clive S. (eds.), *Hannah Arendt: Thinking, Judging, Freedom* (Sydney: Allen and Unwin, 1989).

Kateb, George, *Hannah Arendt: Politics, Conscience, Evil* (Oxford: Martin Robertson, 1984).

Kazin, Alfred, *New York Jew* (London: Secker and Warburg, 1978).

May, Derwent, *Hannah Arendt* (Harmondsworth: Penguin, 1986).

Parekh, Bhikhu, *Hannah Arendt and the Search for a New Political Philosophy* (London and Basingstoke: Macmillan, 1981).

Paz, Mizi, 'The Outsider', *Davar* (8 September, 1989), p. 24.

Pells, Richard H., *The Liberal Mind in a Conservative Age: American Intellectuals in the 1940s and 1950s* (Middletown, Conn.: Wesleyan University Press, 1989).

Podhoretz, Norman, 'Hannah Arendt on Eichmann: A Study in the Perversity of Brilliance', *Commentary*, 36:3 (1963), pp. 201-8.

Praxis, 9:1/2, 'Symposium on Hannah Arendt's Political Thought', (1989).

Quinton, Anthony, 'Hannah Arendt', in Bullock, Alan and Woodings, R. B. (eds.), *The Fontana Biographical Companion to Modern Thought* (London: Fontana: 1983), p. 19.

Rabinach, Anson, 'The Jewish Question in the German Question', *New German Critique*, 44 (1988), pp. 159-92.

Robinson, Jacob, *And the Crooked Shall Be Made Straight: The Eichmann Trial, the Jewish Catastrophe, and Hannah Arendt's Narrative* (New York: Macmillan, 1965).

Social Research, 44, special edition on 'Hannah Arendt', (1977).

Smith, Roger W., *Guilt: Man and Society*, includes Arendt's 'Organized Guilt and Universal Responsibility', (Garden City, New York: Anchor Books, 1971).

Voegelin, Eric, 'The Origins of Totalitarianism', *The Review of Politics*, 15 (1953), pp. 68-76.

Whitfield, Stephen J., *Into the Dark: Hannah Arendt and Totalitarianism* (Philadelphia: Temple University Press, 1980).

Wolin, Sheldon, 'Stopping to Think', *New York Review of Books* (26 October 1978), pp. 18–21.

Young-Bruehl, Elisabeth, *Hannah Arendt: For Love of the World* (New Haven and London: Yale University Press, 1982).

Young-Bruehl, Elisabeth, *Mind and the Body Politic* (New York and London: Routledge, 1989).